30130504219805

The Legend of
GARBO

The Legend of
GARBO

PETER
HAINING

SOUTHEND COLLEGE OF TECHNOLOGY
CARNARVON ROAD, SOUTHEND-ON-SEA

W H ALLEN

E200753835200l.

For Philippa—
with love

Copyright © Peter Haining, 1990

Typeset by Phoenix Photosetting, Chatham
Printed and bound in Great Britain
for the Publishers W. H. Allen & Co. PLC
26 Grand Union Centre
338 Ladbroke Grove
London W10 5AH

This book is sold subject to the condition that it shall not, by way of trade or
otherwise, be lent, re-sold, hired out or otherwise circulated without the
publisher's prior consent in any form of binding or cover other than that in
which it is published and without a similar condition including this condition
being imposed upon the subsequent purchaser.

Essex County Library

GZ 50719

791.H3028 HAI

15 April 1990

A LIVING LEGEND has today become immortal.

Just as elusively as she lived, a great actress has slipped beyond the final curtain of death – though death can surely do nothing to diminish the special place she already holds in the history of our times. Behind her she leaves the enigma of her life, as fascinating to her millions of admirers as her ageless beauty and beguiling screen presence.

We shall certainly never see her like again. And so, to mark the passing of one of the true super-stars of the cinema, this volume of the memories and reflections of those who knew and worked with her is offered as a tribute to the one and only – *Garbo*.

Peter Haining

CONTENTS

Alistair Cooke,
THE GUARDIAN

'Garbo is every man's harmless fantasy mistress . . . By being worshipped by the entire world she gives you the feeling that if your imagination has to sin, it can at least congratulate itself on its impeccable taste.'

Campbell Dixon,
DAILY TELEGRAPH

'I would say Garbo is one of the greatest actresses of the world, one of the very few whose passing would leave a great, unfillable void.'

INTRODUCTION

'Except physically, we know little more about Garbo than we know about Shakespeare.'

Kenneth Tynan

It was a sharp, bright day in New York. The cold edge of winter had not yet quite disappeared from the wind gusting through the towering skyscraper blocks of Manhattan, and the light which shafted down onto the busy streets had the harshness of an early Spring sun.

On First Avenue, where I had been shop-window gazing, there was the usual bustle of people and traffic, the sound of motor horns continually piercing the general hubbub. Clouds of steam were rising like wraiths from the manhole covers in the road, occasionally enveloping the lines of pedestrians who hurried across. I stopped at the corner of the junction with East 52nd Street and glanced to my right, as a visitor from England trained to look for traffic from that direction almost automatically does even after days in the city. Down at the end of the tree-lined street, beyond the railings which marked the cul-de-sac over the Franklin Roosevelt Drive, I could see the dark blue of the East River, glinting dully in the sunlight. As I stood there momentarily, a figure passed by me moving down the street. It was an elderly woman, her body wrapped in a padded trouser suit and a woollen hat on her head. A wisp of greyish hair hung from underneath the hat and almost reached her dark glasses.

I was about to cross the road and go on up First Avenue when *something* made me hesitate. I looked at the old lady again. She *seemed* just like any other elderly New Yorker. But my mind insisted there was something about her that was familiar. Was it her walk? It was measured and rather dignified, despite her age. Or her face? It was lined, certainly, but there was something about its shape and features. The eyes, perhaps? From what I had glimpsed behind the dark glasses, they were dark and languid, with very long eyelashes.

The Eyes. That was it. I suddenly – for no apparent reason – recalled a piece of poetry that I had read years ago:

'Deep lustrous pools of sapphire rare,
    Wherein a realm of beauty lies,
And swooping shadows hover there,
    To veil the wonder of the eyes.'

It was a piece of high-flown doggerel to be sure: but because it referred to someone I admired on the cinema screen, it had somehow registered itself in my subconscious to reemerge at this moment in time. Why, I asked myself, was this old lady walking slowly up a block in busy Manhattan the person I *thought* she might be?

I checked the number of the street and followed her. She walked the length of the road and then hesitated under the awning of the very last apartment block, an almost Gothic-like building with an uninterrupted view across the East River. Two old-fashioned lamps hung on either side of the dark blue cupola which bore the figures '450'.

Then she turned, as if somehow aware she was being followed, and for just an instant our eyes met. My heart skipped a beat. A moment more and she had disappeared into the building. I walked by the ornately iron-barred windows and peered into the entrance. In the foyer I saw the letter 'G' above one of the mailboxes. I *had* been right.

I knew then for sure that for a short space of time – no more than a few minutes – I had been close to the person once described as "the most beautiful woman in the world". The actress who had left the screen at the height of her fame over forty years before and become a recluse, an enigma, and, perhaps most of all, a legend in her own lifetime.

Garbo.

I had known, long before, that the Swedish-born actress had chosen to make her home in New York. But as a person who had 'wanted to be alone' – as she was frequently quoted to have said – it seemed such an unlikely place. But therein lay the paradox, of course. For just as Garbo never actually said she wished to be alone – what she said was that she wanted to be *'left* alone' – so she had realised that it was easier to be anonymous in the heart of one of the most populous cities in the world than it would be on some island or remote estate, positively inviting inquisitive sightseers and preying photographers.

So what had happened to me had been an almost million-to-one chance. Oh, certainly, I might have hung around the neighbourhood as tourists and photographers had done over the years hoping to catch a glimpse of her on one of her walks. But Garbo the hunted had learned through bitter experience how to avoid her hunters, and as you will find by talking to those who live in the area, her privacy is respected and her walks never interrupted.

I wish now, though, that I had been bold enough to try and say *something* to her. One does not come into the presence of a legend very often in one's lifetime, and even the kind of rebuff she gave to a persistent journalist enquiring about a rumoured romance way back in 1931 would have been worthwhile to have heard that unmistakable, resonant voice.

'Do you know a Mr Anderson of Sweden?' the reporter is supposed to have enquired.

'Do you,' the story says she replied, 'know a Mr Smith of the United States?'

What has seemed to many people like an obsessive, life-long quest for absolute privacy on Garbo's part, which transformed her from a film goddess to a hermit in New York's steel caverns, predictably only increased the interest in her. For her screen performances were not those of any ordinary actress: nor was her fame built on clever publicity or brilliant promotion as is so often the case with modern film stars. She genuinely illuminated the silent and talking pictures in which she appeared – whatever their merits – and this unique talent is evident to even the most casual viewer, four decades and more after the films were made. Time has done nothing to diminish their impact – and timeless, indeed, her screen presence has proved to be.

But the great irony of her life is that *if* Garbo had faded away gradually with a decreasing number of pictures in the normal manner, instead of disappearing from the screen so suddenly and so permanently, the anonymity she sought would certainly have been hers whether she desired it or not. Instead, as many an observer has remarked, the interest and controversy surrounding Garbo became unending. By hiding, she became more than ever in sight: feeding the world's curiosity by her non-appearance. Alone she might have chosen to be – but 'left alone' – never!

She has done nothing whatsoever to promote her legend – nothing, that is, beyond remaining determinedly elusive. The most enchantingly mysterious woman of her time to her millions of admirers, she is caught in a time warp of the thirties which is for ever being repeated when her films are shown around the world.

Her screen image has been endlessly examined, but never truly explained, for somehow she expresses something individual to each viewer. Many have tried to explain this magic – film-maker, Billy Wilder, for instance, who said; 'Her face is amazing. It has such uniqueness, such luminosity that it touches everyone. You read into it what you like.' Or critic Jean George Auriol who defined it in a way I find very satisfying when he wrote: 'Have you ever thought of the emotions let loose in the cinema's darkness when the countenance of Greta Garbo assumes possession of the screen? What waves of love, jealousy, regrets, hatred, pity, renunciation, complaisance, immediately reverberate among, and cross-infect, the spectator?'

I am not sure personally that we should like it if her mystery ever *were* completely explained, although this book sets out to try and offer some explanations through observations by people close to her during her working life. Mystery is indeed the very essence of her appeal on the screen and it seems encapsulated in her very name, Garbo, chosen apparently by her mentor, the Swedish director Mauritz Stiller, as being more suitable than her given names of Greta Gustafsson.

Though an explanation has been offered as to how Stiller arrived at the name – it is said to be a derivation of King Gabor of Hungary – I like to believe that this is rather too commonplace an idea for our first lady of the screen. For if we consult Swedish mythology we can discover there details about a mysterious Scandinavian sprite which comes out at night to dance in the moonbeams. By day it withdraws to its land of dreams. This sprite is called a Garbon.

Doesn't this expression perfectly describe Garbo? Isn't what she does before our eyes in a darkened cinema dancing on moonbeams: a kind of 'Garboning' as the mythology describes the sprite's activities? That seems far more likely to me to be the origin of her name – a name now so familiar it requires no explanation, no elaboration. Yet how does one explain a life that burned so brightly, so quickly, and then so suddenly became all silence? For forty years she answered all enquiries about her plans with the response: 'Plans? I have no plans. I'm sort of drifting.' And indeed what words could more precisely

The incomparably beautiful Garbo in Mata Hari *(1932)*

describe her lifestyle since she gave up her career at the age of thirty-six and at the very height of her powers?

There are those who think fondly of the beautiful things she might have done for the screen; others who chastise her for having wasted much more than half her adult life. Yet publicly she has never shown herself to be anything other than content with this state of affairs. A naturally lazy streak in her make-up plus the wealth she earned and then shrewdly invested, has left her with no pressures to do anything other than what *she* wants. Melancholy she may often have appeared, restless to a degree, but friendless never – although those who were admitted to her small circle had to learn that they must never speak of her publicly unless they wished to suffer instant banishment.

This desire to prevent details of her life appearing has played a major part in the general lack of real information about her – though it has instigated an unending stream of words about her. Where, I hope, this book differs from its predecessors is that it contains the statements and observations of fellow professionals in the cinema business. Some were written in order to try to put right the multitude of erroneous stories that were written about her; others out of sheer admiration for her talent. Regrettably, many cost the authors their friendship with Garbo (though it is not often easy to see why), but we should be grateful for their sacrifice because of the light they throw on this most enigmatic lady. I should add that most have not previously been republished since their original magazine or newspaper publication.

In collecting these essays from many and varied sources, I came to realise that Garbo is exactly what we believe the archetypal film star should be – remote, lustrous, inaccessible, infinitely removed from anything ordinary. As Billy Wilder has again explained; 'It may be the goddamest put-on of all time, yet Garbo is the quintessence of what a star should be. Today's actresses tell us how they bring up their children and give us their recipe for scrambled eggs, but Garbo stumbled on a much more compelling idea. She said and did nothing and let the world write her story. She was as incongruous in Hollywood as Sibelius would have been if he had come to write incidental music for Warner Brothers films.'

If we think about it for a moment, who else among the stars of the screen has come even remotely near her? There are, of course, those who argue that memories of Garbo play tricks. That what sustains her legend are just a

lot of old film stills and some fading prints of her pictures which do not really stand re-examination. Yet look again at the best of her work and see. In *Flesh and the Devil*, *Camille* and *Ninotchka*, for instance, she is undeniably vital and warm-blooded: revealing herself to be a superb actress *as well as* a peerless screen image. Older fans who were around when her pictures were first shown may well claim her spell is truly enshrined only in their hearts, yet talk to younger generations who have discovered Garbo in their turn through film festivals or on television . . .

'She's so lovely and romantic,' one teenage girl told me at a recent festival. 'And that face. What a marvellous, marvellous face.' And another enthused, 'There's something so refined and graceful about her films. I get so sick of all these naked film lovers rolling about in modern movies.' It is quite evident that Garbo's mysterious magic formula works on this generation just as it had done on those before. And it is of such quality that I am sure it will continue to endure for generations to come.

As I said earlier, I become less sure as the years pass that we really need to try and explain what her secret was, despite all the attempts to do so. The twentieth century has been an age obsessed with visual images, and hers was surely the face and personality which exactly suited her time. Nor do I think we need to seek for comparisons between the public and private person, for as Cecil Beaton who enjoyed an ill-fated friendship with her has most revealingly written: 'She is as beautiful as the aurora borealis, but to compare Garbo on and off the screen is to compare de Laszlo with Leonardo. The personality the public see is magnetic, gay, tragic, sensitive and wise; but other actresses appear magnetic and sensitive, until the projector stops, and the illusion created by the director and his aides is dispelled. Only Garbo, when the properties are back in the box, puts on nobility with her mackintosh. In real life, she possesses such a wealth of qualities, which the screen is technically incapable of reproducing, that even if she had not the most beautiful face of our time, all other modern beauty would be ephemeral beside hers.'

This book is not meant to be a sensational or prying work – more a memorial to a great actress in which the voices of those who knew and worked and loved her speak more loudly and, I believe, more authentically, than the opinions of any single biographer with all his prejudices and preconceived ideas. To be sure there are ques-

18

tions left unanswered, but these can only be answered by the subject herself and she never will.

Though she stopped acting all those years ago, Garbo's life itself may almost be seen in hindsight to have been her greatest role. Biographer Norman Zierold put his finger on this aspect when he wrote in 1970: 'That fact is that Garbo, world symbol of the charismatic loner, has virtually done everything, gone everywhere, seen everyone. She has managed to live her own richly peopled life while simultaneously retaining her mystique, assuring its survival long after her departure from films. The feat constitutes one of the bravura performances of our time.'

I have tried, in the pages which follow, to highlight the most important scenes from her amazing life: a few recorded in Garbo's own words, but in the main by others who shared her stage for a time. I offer the book as a tribute, aware that the central mystery still remains as impenetrable as ever. Ramon Novarro the actor has expressed my feelings precisely when he said almost twenty years ago: 'Did Garbo invent herself? Did publicity invent her? It was meant to be. Garbo was mysterious without trying.'

Peter Haining
London

TRIBUTES TO GARBO

Lars Hanson

(1880–1956)

Appeared with Garbo in The Story of Gösta Berling (*1924*), Flesh and the Devil (*1927*) *and* The Divine Woman (*1928*)

'Playing with Greta was pleasurable work. She was so sincere, so serious, so selflessly devoted to the perfect delineation of the character she was portraying. This allowed work to go on wonderfully well.

'Besides, there was, how do you say, a sympathy, an understanding between us, for were we not of the same soil, speaking the same language, and from the same country? This makes for a huge difference between an actor and actress.

'We also both owed much to Mauritz Stiller and Victor Seastrom, having worked with them in Sweden as well as in America. Indeed, Garbo only came to Hollywood because Stiller, who had discovered her, insisted on having her along if he was to sign a contract with MGM.'

Picturegoer, June 1929

John Gilbert

(1895–1936)

Lars Hanson with Garbo in Flesh and the Devil *(1927)*

Overleaf: John Gilbert and Garbo in Queen Christina *(1933)*

Starred with Garbo in Flesh and the Devil (*1927*), Love (*1927*), A Woman of Affairs (*1929*), Queen Christina (*1933*)

'Garbo is just a gay, simple country girl at heart, putting on a mantle that did not really belong to her because she suffered from agonising shyness.

'She can also be the most alluring creature you have ever seen. Capricious as the devil, whimsical, temperamental and fascinating. When she doesn't feel like working, she will not work. Garbo never acts unless she feels she can do herself justice.

'But what magnetism when she gets in front of the camera! What appeal! What a woman! One day she is childlike, naive, ingenuous, a girl of ten. The next day, she is a mysterious woman a thousand years old, knowing everything, baffling, deep. Garbo has more sides to her personality than anyone I have ever met.

'You should hear Greta laugh, though, when she's really happy. Then you would know more about what she is really like. I remember sometimes when she was up at my house, after we had all been fooling around in the pool or on the tennis court, I would see her sneaking off to a corner and putting on that air of gloom and mystery all of a sudden.

'So I would rush over to her, give her a shake, a good hard slap on the back, and tell her to snap out of it. I would grab her arm and steer her to the edge of the pool – one quick push, and she would be in the water, spluttering, splashing, shouting with laughter. And when she came out, shaking her head like a spaniel, *then* the real, natural Greta was with us again.

'There is something eternal about her. Not only did she baffle me, but she baffled everyone at the studio. Once, she had been missing for days and I went to see her. Her maid told me she had gone to the beach. I jumped in my car and motored for miles way out beyond Santa Monica. I found her at last. She was all alone and just coming out of the surf. She didn't see me so I watched her to see what she would do. She stood on the beach all by herself and just looked out at the ocean for fifteen minutes. She seemed really content – just standing alone watching the ocean.' *Screen Book Magazine*, December 1932

Nils Asther

(1902–81)

Appeared with Garbo in Wild Orchids (*1929*), The Single Standard (*1929*)

'Like Greta Garbo I have been given many labels by the newspapers and magazines. ''Very nearly as handsome as

Valentino," one writer has said. And "the masculine version of that mysterious fascination that is Garbo's", declares another. In fact, I am tired of being just a screen lover, and I hope some day to get a chance to be myself.

'I am rather like Greta in that I like to be alone. I love peace and quiet. Hollywood is really no place for me. I stagnate there.

'It is easy to become idle in the warm sun and hot air of Los Angeles. But that is shameful, for idleness does not suit me. I only really feel awake when the air is fresh and crisp as in my native Scandinavia. I believe it is because Garbo is from Sweden that she also feels the same. Maybe one day she will escape from Hollywood and work in Europe again as I plan to do.'

Picture Show, October 1935

Clark Gable
(1901–60)

Appeared with Garbo in Susan Lennox: Her Fall and Rise (*1931*).

'I was tremendously interested in working with Greta Garbo in *Susan Lennox* and I enjoyed watching her when I was not in a scene. I must admit that I learned very little from her, however, for though I studied her carefully, I never found out what it was that she did. If I had found out it probably wouldn't have helped me at all, for Garbo is a law unto herself. The things she does are absolutely right for her, but who else could do them?

'She is a very glamorous person, but it is easy to work with her. I wasn't nervous, as other men say they are, when I was in a scene with her, but I was deeply interested. In fact, I found my work easier than usual, but this was partly because Garbo works from nine to five only!

'It was from a woman with whom I have never played that I learned most about acting. I mean Maria Dressler. I have watched her pictures with the keenest interest, noting carefully how she times or spaces her every move, speech and gesture to get the maximum effectiveness. Timing or spacing, as we call it in the studio, is important in any dramatic action. You can imagine, then, with what interest I approached my work with Garbo having seen

Nils Asther with Garbo in Wild Orchids *(1929)*

Clark Gable and Garbo in Susan Lennox: Her Fall and Rise *(1931)*

her give such a splendid performance the previous year in *Anna Christie* in which Maria Dressler also starred. I think that film will long remain one of my favourites.'

Picturegoer, June 1934

Ramon Novarro
(1899–1968)

Starred with Garbo in Mata Hari (1932).

'Greta Garbo is unique. Every scene she does has to be developed in herself. She *means* whatever she is doing for the time being. Every scene is very real to her. That is why she has a reputation for being moody – a person apart from the rest. She cannot help that. Every part she plays is an emotional experience for her.

'During the filming of *Mata Hari*, Garbo always wanted to rehearse the love scenes with me in private. She needed to be able to concentrate. She had to convince herself before she could convince anyone else.

'I liked Garbo very much, although it seems to me she was impersonal. I don't think she was ever in love with anyone. Someone must have frightened her at the very beginning.'

Daily Mail, January 1950

Ramon Novarro with Garbo in Mata Hari *(1932)*

26

Lionel Barrymore

(1878–1954)

Appeared with Garbo in The Temptress (*1926*), Mata Hari (*1931*), Grand Hotel (*1932*) *and* Camille (*1937*).

'Garbo is simple. This, to me, is her greatest quality. She's also extraordinarily dextrous. She has a very powerful personality which gives her command in everything she does, but she never depends on it, doesn't consider it a particular asset. What she does consider is that acting is her job, and she keeps everlastingly at it.

'It is because she is so completely simple that Garbo bears the unmistakable mark of greatness. Modjeska had it, that same simplicity, so that when she came on the stage you expected to see the theatre catch fire. Ellen Terry was another who made it felt, a sudden arrestation, a strange power that held you.

'Garbo has only to flash on the screen to seize our attention. Her very brilliance dispels our dullness. She takes us out of ourselves into another realm by the mere accident of her presence. It isn't acting; it has nothing to do with

Lionel Barrymore and Garbo in Camille (*1937*)

acting; it is something which holds us in its spell – a kind of magic. This magic is in Garbo.

'Garbo is great to work with. She is always right. With her you never have any trouble about knowing what to do. She comes right back at you every time, like mental tennis. But she hates to be interrupted, won't stand any outside interference. It doesn't matter who tries to break in on her working hours.

'Although she has the true nimbus of greatness, she is extremely shy. I think that the gods in meting out their gifts neglected to endow her with small talk.'

Sunday Chronicle, November 1937

John Barrymore
(1882–1942)

Brother of Lionel, appeared with Garbo in Grand Hotel *(1932).*

'When I acted with Garbo in *Grand Hotel* I found that she was not as cold and aloof as people said, but rather shy. A little bit like myself, in fact. But she responded to my humour.

John Barrymore with Garbo in Grand Hotel *(1932)*

'On the set we both talked mainly about acting and other actors while we waited to be called. I remember that she mentioned one actor she thought was particularly good. "There are no good actors," I told her. "There are only bad ones who try to make themselves and others think they are good. Some can bring it off; others can't."

'There were moments during the film when I sensed she was a bit unsure about her work. On one occasion I whispered to her just before a take, "You're the most enchanting person in the world." She responded beautifully. As soon as the scene was over, she threw her arms round me and thanked me, praising my skill as an actor.

'Garbo herself is a great lady and a great actress – and, the rest is silence.'

Film Weekly, February 1938

Fredric March
(1897–1975)

Starred with Garbo in Anna Karenina (*1935*).

'I think Garbo is the greatest tragedy of Hollywood. She lives a life that would be a terrific mental and physical strain on anyone. And becoming an extreme introvert has been her means of building up a wall of protection for herself. I had a personal and rather uncomfortable experience of this "Garbo wall" during the filming of *Anna Karenina*. As we were acting an intimate scene together, she suddenly noticed my stand-in about fifteen to twenty feet away watching the action. At once she asked me, "Does it not bother you to have people watching you while you work?" I replied, "Why, no. Anyway, that's just my stand-in. He wants to be an actor and he likes to watch." Garbo was silent for a few moments and then she said, "Mr March, I do not think you understand me." At this I said, "What do you mean?"

'"It bothers *me*," she said, "to have people I do not know watching me." I apologised to her, of course, but it was with a feeling that I was being awfully silly.

'On another occasion, I stood behind some scenery watching Garbo do a scene alone. When she had finished I walked over to compliment her on a nice piece of work. To my surprise she immediately replied, "Oh, you should not have done that. You are a naughty boy. It troubles me

to have people watch me." And this was the woman I had had in my arms in a love scene only the day before!'

Los Angeles Mirror, August 1954

Charles Boyer
(1897–1978)

Appeared with Garbo in Conquest (*1937*).

'From my earliest recollections I was in love with one small mademoiselle or another. Later boyhood years did not change me. In my native town, Figeac, in France, boys and girls didn't go to school together. So I guess from the beginning girls were a mystery to me, and in my childish fancy they were created to be fallen in love with. Their faces are all blurred now in my memory, but later ones I can remember. There was a very beautiful girl who came to teach philosophy in our school. I worshipped her with boyish admiration, which I'm perfectly certain she was never conscious of.

'I rather felt, therefore, that I was well prepared to play Napoleon in *Conquest*. And, of course, any Frenchman would naturally regard it as a high honour and a great responsibility to play him. I tried to depict Napoleon, the man, as he was. Garbo was the ideal choice for the role of Countess Walewska. And in France, where they idolise her, I know that the picture made screen history.

'As a matter of interest, I actually owe the culmination of my romance with Pat Paterson to Greta Garbo. Pat and I were planning to attend the premiere of *Queen Christina* at the Chinese Theatre. When we arrived, every seat had been taken. As we stood in the lobby, I said, "Let's be married – immediately!" So we flew to Yuma, and within an hour we were married.'

Picturegoer, April 1938

Melvyn Douglas
(1901–81)

Appeared with Garbo in As You Desire Me (*1932*), Ninotchka (*1939*) *and her last film*, Two-Faced Woman (*1941*).

'I could not have had a better introduction to the movies, for in my first film I was paired with Gloria Swanson, and

Previous Page: *Fredric March and Garbo in* Anna Karenina (*1935*)

Charles Boyer with Garbo in Conquest (*1937*)

32

in the second with Greta Garbo. The Garbo film was *As You Desire Me*, a modern version of Pirandello's play, and she was then at the very peak of her art and her fame. Without any doubt, that film assured me of success as a screen actor. I learned a great deal from working with her and thereafter my admiration for her was unqualified.

'Although Garbo laughing for the first time on the screen in *Ninotchka* in that drinking scene with me caused such interest, I had often seen her smile before. Generally, her personality was happy whenever she felt secure and not under pressure. I also know, however, that she was unhappy about *Two-Faced Woman*, our third film together, right from the start. MGM were trying to make her into a typical American glamour girl, cutting her hair into a bob, and getting her to wear a bathing suit and wispy finery. I remember she said to me while we were filming, ''They're trying to kill me.'' And, as you know, immediately it was released, *Two-Faced Woman* ran into trouble with the Catholic Church. They said it had an immoral and un-Christian attitude towards marriage. So MGM made changes. Garbo was very depressed about the way things turned out with that picture and I believe it was one of the reasons why she never filmed again.'

Photoplay, August 1976

Melvyn Douglas and Garbo in As You Desire Me *(1932)*

Greta Garbo
MY LIFE AS AN ARTIST

The infant destined to grow into the legendary Garbo was born Greta Lovisa Gustafsson on 18 September, 1905 in the Södra Maternity Hospital, Stockholm, the beautiful capital city of Sweden. Her father, Karl Alfred Gustafsson, had a menial job working as a street cleaner for the local authority, which did little for his poor health and led to his death when Greta was only fourteen. Her mother, Anna Lovisa, was a much sturdier soul of Lapp extraction, who had grown up on a farm and worked as a kitchen maid until the time of her marriage. The Gustafssons had three children: a son, Sven, a daughter, Alva Maria, and Greta, the youngest, and all were raised in a pokey, unpretentious apartment flat at 32 Blekingegatan. The family all slept in one room, cooking was done over a small stove, and along with the other tenants they shared a lavatory situated in the courtyard. This courtyard was the only place for youngsters like Greta to play.

Because of Karl Gustafsson's weak constitution and untimely death, the children knew the meaning of hardship from their infancy and only the tireless effort and resolution of Anna Lovisa kept the little family together. Greta's admiration and affection for her mother was, as she once admitted, 'beyond mere words'. There has naturally been much speculation about Garbo's early life, and each biographer in the past has presented his own version of these formative years. I have been particularly fortunate, however, in being able to locate an essay which Greta Garbo herself wrote about this period of her life. It was written in 1930, when she was just just twenty-four years old, in conjunction with a young man named Lars Saxon, the editor of a Swedish magazine named *Lektyr*.

Saxon had originally met Greta while she was filming her first major picture, *The Story of Gösta Berling*, in 1924, and they were to remain friends until his death in 1950. 'My Life as an Artist', which is here translated into English for the first time, is an ideal contribution with which to begin this volume, since Greta gives us her own version of her youth, and how events transpired that were to draw her into the world of films and, ultimately, take her to Hollywood . . .

The fledgling actress about to conquer the world

Overleaf: *Garbo in* The Street of Sorrow *(1925)*

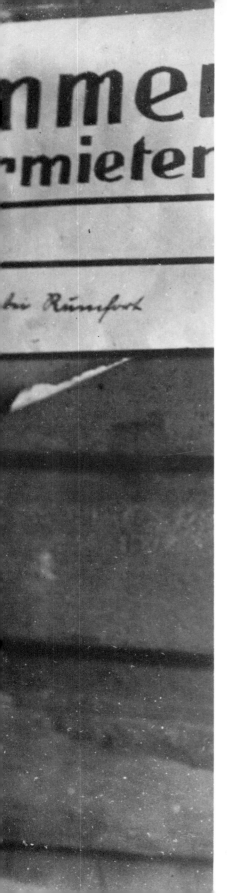

Six years ago I was an ordinary, unknown teenager living in Stockholm, the city where I was born. My name was Greta Gustafsson. Now I am twenty-four years old and my life is very different indeed . . .

When I look back on the road I have travelled, I am not as surprised as I expect to be, for each event in my life seems to have developed so naturally from the preceding one that despite the difference between the point of departure and arrival, the transition has seemed imperceptible. But the story of this travel is what interests you, I believe: the story of my life, in fact.

But when we stop to think, don't we all do the same things? We go to school, we learn, we grow, we change. Some more so than others. Some are born in beautiful houses, others in poor homes: but for the long journey that lies ahead none of that is really very important. It is only gradually that we discover our true aim in life. Then we try to attain it, and our work is the evidence of our efforts. Mine happens to be in the world of films . . .

Please don't be surprised to hear me talk like this. Bear with me for a moment. Remember that I am a Scandinavian, and while I may admire the astonishing vitality and happy, extrovert temperament of the American women with whom I have come in contact, I cannot imitate them. I know I have been thought of as proud and disdainful, but I am not. It is more a sort of reserve, which is as natural to me as liveliness is to others!

I have always been a little inclined to be melancholy. As a child, I loved to sit in a corner and dream. I hate crowds and noise. I remember my mother used to say, 'Go out and play!' But the idea didn't appeal, and I am now of the opinion that it is much more sensible to leave children

39

alone, to let them play and dream as they please, and build up a world which is all their own. That is better than any organised game.

One thing I loved as a child was skating. Skimming madly through the keen, cold air, while the wind whistles in your ears and you feel light – light and swift – that is a marvellous sensation. In fact all the winter sports of my country attracted me. I excelled at them and they made me happy. Along with my enchanted world of dreams they filled my life.

But the harsh world of reality was not slow in forcing an entry into my pleasures. At fourteen, I lost my father. It is terrible to see someone you love torn from you like that for ever. But I shall not dwell on it.

I was the youngest of the family. My brother, Sven, was the eldest and he, too, wanted to be a film actor. My sister, Alva, was three years older and a true friend to me. She was lively, gay, happy and beautiful – much more so than I. She, too, had made a start in films and I visualised a successful future for her which would have brought the whole family happiness. But tragedy struck us once more and she died. I was far away in America when this happened and I can still scarcely believe it is true.

And my mother? She was just Mother and the centre of my life . . .

Although I was the youngest in the family, they all somehow regarded me as the eldest! That was probably because of my serious and thoughtful character. I had very decided ideas about things – sometimes with no real reason for such ideas – and often they used to come to me before making decisions or to help resolve a problem. I suppose my main fault at this time lay in my excessively changeable nature. At one moment I would be happy and cheerful, the next plunged in sorrow and depression.

On looking back, I realise that early in my life one thing became very clear to me: I had a passion for the theatre. I was born with it. None of my family had ever been on the stage, but from childhood I loved to make myself up and devise my own little dramas. I would act these with my brother and sister. Sometimes I was an evil spirit, spreading ruination and death in my wake. My sister would kill herself out of jealousy, my brother out of despair. I only smiled! On other occasions I would sacrifice myself totally, desperately, to bring happiness to the one I loved. As you can see, I had a very romantic imagination for a child!

When I was about eight, a very important event occur-

Greta's mother . . .

. . . and father

red in my life. I had taken to hiding every evening under the porch of the Southside Theatre, to watch the comings and goings of the actors. Then I would run home, where I was invariably scolded for being late! Yet the strange thing was that I never thought of standing by the front entrance. It was always the stage door that made my heart beat with a kind of longing . . . and hope. Then, one evening, I took courage and slipped inside. There I could see the actors hurrying about their business, and for the first time I breathed that marvellous smell – so beloved of theatre addicts! – a mixture of make-up and powder, of sweat and dust. No smell in the world has a richer meaning!

It was not until I was twelve, however, that I entered a theatre for the first time as a spectator, perched up high in the gods. The Southside Theatre stood on a hill, and from there one could also look down on the town. How many times did I lean over to gaze on the panorama below? In the darkness the lights sparkled, giving the world a magical look.

Such were my best moments. School? I didn't like it! I felt oppressed and unhappy there. But I did enjoy history, literature and music, although I developed a profound hatred for geography. I just could not understand maps at all. Even recreation in the playground did not appeal to me. I only wanted one thing: the end of the school day which meant escape, home and liberty.

The theatre was not the only thing in my life – there was also the cinema. I can't remember the first time I went, but like most children I went as often as I could. There was one near our home, and as the owner knew me and was a kind man at heart, he often let me in without paying. That was very lucky, because I rarely had any money . . .

The death of my father changed the entire pattern of our existence. My mother was left alone with three children. The two eldest had left school, so they could go to work. I longed to finish, too, so that I could find some sort of job. However, during my last days at school, I discovered a means of earning a few *kroner*. I will tell you about it, although I must say there was nothing very romantic about the work. My job was helping a barber in the neighbourhood by lathering the chins of his customers! You may well smile at that when you think of some of the glamorous things I have done since! At the time I was tall and well-built for my age although I was only fourteen. I was very unhappy about my figure, and I was clumsy and gangling – just a big girl who had grown too fast. As soon as I finished school I continued to work at the barber's for a short while. Then, one day, I decided to take advantage of my mature appearance by applying for a job at the big department store of Paul U. Bergström. They listened to me, looked me over and took my name and address. That was all – and I walked home feeling very sad. But a few days later I received a letter asking me to call again. I remember that I ran all the way!

I was engaged in the ladies' hats department as a sales girl. And soon after it was time to display the new spring models. To my delight I was asked to act as a mannequin in presenting the new lines. Apparently my head suited the hats. Later a photographer came in to take some pictures of me, and that spring and summer the Bergström catalogues had portraits of me displaying the smartest hats in the store! Whatever you may think, I really *was* interested in selling hats. It was a bit like a game. You had to know how to handle each customer. Somehow, it came quite naturally to me. Even though I was now working, I still kept my great love for the theatre. How I admired the actresses who came to the store. How I envied them.

Only occasionally did I have the chance to visit a show, and more often than not I came away disappointed. The actors did not inspire me and the plays, too, seemed far removed from the marvellous dramas I had dreamed about – those lively, romantic works of my own imagination. Although I did not realise it at the time, I was already beginning to formulate my own ideas on the art of acting.

My First Film

One day, the hat department was suddenly thrown into a turmoil. The publicity manager of Bergström came to see us, accompanied by a large, smiling man. His name was Captain Ragnar Ring, and he was the director of a Swedish company that made advertising films. The news got around like wildfire. The store was to make a film showing the public how it could dress them from head to foot. Real actors and actresses would play the main roles, but it was possible there might be small parts for the sales girls.

Captain Ring took a few notes and was just about to leave when the publicity manager stopped him. 'There is a girl here who modelled some hats for us,' he said, pointing at me. 'Perhaps we could use her?'

I felt my heart beating fit to burst. Captain Ring looked at me. 'I'm sorry,' he said, 'but our star Olga Anderson will do very well for the hats.'

The two men walked away. I was naturally disappointed, but I did still get a bit-part. We began rehearsals a few days later. I had to wear a riding outfit which was deliberately too big for me. I had to go through some comical poses in this in front of a mirror. When I had finished, the producer congratulated me, and assured me that I had been fine. Such was my very first screen appearance. Captain Ring was satisfied with my work and promised me some more in other advertising films. He soon kept his promise. The following year, in fact, he gave me a small part in a film demonstrating the workings of a bakery.

That same year, 1922, I was offered a part in a full-length film of a Nordic love story which was to be shot on location in the Swedish countryside. What an opportunity for a sixteen-year-old! But, alas, Bergström would not allow me time off to film. I had become invaluable to them both as a sales girl and a model. I was broken-hearted over this disappointment.

Perhaps not surprisingly, the sales job soon ceased to interest me. To someone who dreamed of nothing but the theatre, the little film parts I had played had filled me with hope. I could endure this tedious work no longer, it bored me to death. I felt I *must* act! I knew I should go to a school of dramatic art if ever I hoped to fulfil this ambition, and so I directed all my energies to this end. However, it was the cinema which gave me my chance, my decisive chance, and changed the direction of my life for good.

A producer named Erik A. Petschler was about to make a comedy film, rather in the style of Mack Sennett – but he had neither story nor actors. He had noticed me in the street one day when I stopped in front of a shop. In fact, he had stared so intently at me that I became embarrassed and quickly disappeared into the crowd. But, as I was to learn later, my face had appealed to him. He had been on the point of approaching me to ask if I would accept a part in his film when I had run off. However, we were to meet again. Quite by chance, two days later, he came to Bergström's store, accompanied by two young women from his company, to buy hats. He recognised me but, I learned afterwards, he decided that because of the precarious nature of film-making, there was little chance a sales girl would leave her safe job to act in a film, and so he left without speaking a word. However, one of the young women stayed behind and we got into conversation. She was Tyra Ryman, one of Petschler's favourite actresses,

Garbo's first film appearance in How Not to Dress *(1921)*

Overleaf: *Greta with her co-stars in* Peter the Tramp *(1922)*

43

and she told me who he was and about the film he was planning. I asked her if there was any chance I might be able to get a part. She laughed at this and said she was *sure* I was just what the producer wanted!

At this point in my life, I did one of the boldest things I have ever done. I telephoned Petschler the next day. He gave me an appointment. I went along to see him and he offered me an engagement and a salary on the spot. Although it was very modest, I accepted immediately. There was still one big problem though – my job. First, I tried to defer my holiday dates at Bergström's to coincide with the time the film was to be shot. But they refused point blank. Thereupon I took a major decision: I decided to leave the regular but monotonous life of a sales girl for the uncertain but undoubtedly exciting world of acting. I would give myself whole-heartedly to it. Somewhat nervously that night I told my mother what I had decided. To my delight she encouraged me, telling me I was right, that I knew better than anyone what was good for me.

So I made my first feature film, *Peter the Tramp.* I was hardly noticeable in it, but Petschler was pleased and promised me bigger parts in the future. It was, though, some time before this promise was fulfilled, and as it happened not by him.

Working with real actors had convinced me that I needed some serious dramatic training. So I got an introduction to Frans Enwall, who had been a teacher of dramatic art in Stockholm, and told him about my desire. He listened carefully to what I said, and advised me to apply for entrance to the Royal Dramatic Theatre Academy in the city, where I could work for a scholarship. Entry to the Academy took place by way of an examination in August, and I knew that if I succeeded, my dream was part-way to being fulfilled. But if I failed, that would be the end – for in September I would be seventeen, over the age limit for entry. The prospect was terrifying, and on the day of the examination my knees nearly gave way under me. I don't know how I went into the Academy Theatre.

There were twenty people on the examining body – teachers, actors, critics, and journalists. They sat in the orchestra pit, although they could not be seen from the stage. I felt a little sick as I waited in the wings for my turn. My fate was about to be settled. I felt sure I was going to fail. Then I thought of my mother waiting anxiously at home . . .

At last my turn came. I went to the footlights and spoke my piece. I felt somehow as if I was in a dream. Then as soon as I was back in the wings I fainted! When I came to, I went home without speaking a word to anyone. On the way I was seized by the most violent feelings of remorse. Perhaps, I thought, I had ruined everything by leaving without saying anything. That night passed without a wink of sleep. The next day nothing. I began to feel sure I must have failed. I wondered idly whether I ought to go to Bergström and ask for my old job back. Then, at last, on the third day, I had a telephone call from the school. I had passed! I nearly died of joy. I was going to be a real actress – and soon!

I studied at the Academy for two seasons, 1922–23 and 1923–24. My principal was Gustav Molander, now well-known as a producer, and there were several famous Swedish actors among my teachers. It was a marvellous period in my life. But I was still not without worries, for my family were poor, and in spite of the tuition being free, I had to go without many things. Nevertheless, my mother was full of hope and encouragement, and as my sister and brother were bringing in some money we were able to make ends meet.

I still went to the theatre whenever possible. It was a necessary part of my dramatic education. Besides, my fellow students and I had privilege tickets. We all got on very well together. I remember that after the morning sessions we used to meet for coffee at a nearby bar, and there we had endless discussions. We were young, enthusiastic, full of love and passion for our work. Happy days!

The other students often teased me, kindly, about my greatest fault – I was always late. And because I was never scolded, it became a bad habit. My friends would often laugh among themselves when they saw me come in on tiptoe after the class had begun. Despite this, I was still taken on at the Dramatic Theatre which is a part of the Royal Dramatic Theatre Academy. At last I was going to become a real actress!

Enter Mauritz Stiller

At the Dramatic Theatre I played a number of minor roles in the months which followed. I was fairly successful as Hermione in *A Winter's Tale* and I had a small part in *The Invisible Man* by Per Lagerkvist. I also made an appearance in a Schnitzler comedy, *A Farewell Supper*.

One day I received a brief message at the Academy

instructing me not to make any plans for the summer. It was an order which I instantly obeyed when I saw from whom the message came. For it was signed Mauritz Stiller – Stiller, the greatest film-maker in Sweden.

Let me pause here for a moment to reflect on Stiller. To me, his name means everything – he was the cause of all my success, it was thanks to him that I went to America. I not only admired him enormously but grew to hold him in the deepest affection. When he died suddenly in 1928 after we had gone through so much together, I felt an over-whelming sorrow. These are things that I cannot forget. Having said that, let me return to those past days when he was a great man in Sweden.

It was in the Spring of 1923 when I got the message that Stiller was looking for a girl for a new film he was about to embark upon. So that very day, after school, I went to see him. I had never met him before and naturally I was very excited at the prospect.

Stiller was not at home when I arrived, so I had to wait. I grew more and more anxious as I sat there, until finally he came in, accompanied by a big dog which never left his side. I could feel myself trembling. Without so much as a greeting, he stared at me for a long time – a very long time. Later, he was to tell me precisely what I was wearing that day, so carefully had he studied me. At length, after this long silence, he began to talk to me about quite inconse-quential matters, such as the weather, the state of the country, and so on. All the time I felt he was scrutinising me. Suddenly, he asked me to take off my coat and hat. Then he asked me for my telephone number – and that was all.

It seemed obvious to me that I didn't interest him. I put on my coat and hat again, murmured 'Goodbye', and left. I was disappointed, but not annoyed. On reflection, at that time the only thing that mattered to me was to earn money; I wanted to find a job for the summer. So I tried not to think any more about it.

Then, out of the blue a few days later, the phone rang. It was Stiller. 'Will you come to Rasunda Studios tomorrow for a screentest?' he asked. Would I!

So off I went to the studios of Swenska Films accompa-nied by one of my student friends, Mona Martensson, who was also having a screentest. I remember how ner-vous I felt. When we arrived, we were both made up on the set. Stiller pointed to a bed. I was to lie on it, he said, and appear to be very ill. I thought that sounded very

Royal Dramatic Theatre in Stockholm where Garbo first studied acting

47

silly. Stiller watched me for a while. 'Good heavens,' he exclaimed, 'don't you know what it is like to be very ill?'

I tried hard to understand what he wanted. I did my best – but at the end of the test I went home bewildered and miserable. So you can imagine how amazed I was to receive notice a few days later that he wanted me for an important role in *The Story of Gösta Berling*. It was almost unbelievable. I was wildly happy. This new film was already being much talked about in acting circles, and a great deal was expected of it. And I had a marvellous part in it!

I was then eighteen. I was about to work under the direction of a man whom I admired profoundly. And I was to play a role very much after my own heart. You cannot imagine the excitement I still feel even now when I think back to that moment.

For the first few days of filming I was so frightened I couldn't do a thing, It was making me ill. Then Stiller had the idea of clearing almost everyone from the set, while he remained in a corner. I felt easier then. The work progressed slowly. During the summer we filmed the interiors, because for all the outdoor sequences we needed the winter snows. Gradually my fear left me, although I have to confess that I am still anxious and nervous when I am acting. At such times I do not like to be disturbed. I live the part I am playing. I am completely under its spell, so that if anyone tries to talk to me or ask questions, it wakes me up, so to speak.

It was during the filming of *Gösta Berling* that Stiller gave me my theatrical name: and from Greta Gustafsson I became Greta Garbo.

When filming was completed, I found myself in another quandry. I had a contract with the Dramatic Theatre for more stage work, but Stiller wanted me to film again. It did not take me long to make up my mind which way to go, and I cancelled my contract to turn all my attention to the screen.

Gösta Berling scored a great success in Europe. Stiller's genius was applauded once more, and the elements of passion and tenderness, violence and lyricism which had made his earlier picture *Sir Arne's Treasure* so unforgettable were discerned again by the critics.

And this was the man who had faith in me! Stiller said he always let himself be guided by his instinct as this usually led him straight to the actor he needed for any particular part. He allowed no one to influence him. It was of

Mona Martensson, Greta's young actress friend who screen-tested with her

Right: *Mauritz Stiller*

his own accord that he had approached me. 'You will be a great artist,' he declared. I am so glad for his sake, more than my own, that time has proved his intuition right.

Every mention of his name brings memories flooding back. Was he not the first European producer to use the close-up, to employ a mobile camera, and introduce a whole new range of angles for his shots? Above all, though, he had tremendous enthusiasm. The word impossible was unknown to him. He could motivate anyone. Yet, despite his genius and his friends, he was a lonely soul. When we went to America where he made three films – of which *Imperial Hotel* is surely a masterpiece – it hurt me deeply to see him find it impossible to adapt. And so he returned to Sweden, leaving me heartbroken at his failure. For Stiller to fail – he who was so rich in talent – while I his pupil succeeded, seemed so cruel! But there was nothing I could do. Later, when I learned that he was sick and alone, I begged him to let his friends take care of him. But he refused. He would not let anyone see the ravages of his illness.

When a mutual friend, Victor Sjöstrom, who was also working in America, went on holiday to Stockholm, he did manage to see him and give him my affectionate regards. But Victor could see the end was near. And my greeting proved also to be a farewell: the last message he received in this world. It was a message of gratitude from one who owed everything to him and yet had been unable to do anything in return.

But to come back to my story, for I have allowed myself to be carried away by memories. Let us go back to the time when I did not know great fame – nor did I know such great grief.

What the Future Held

It was summertime . . . and I was on holiday in the countryside with my family wondering what the future held for me. One evening I received a letter from Stiller, in which he asked me to go to the premiere of *Gösta Berling* in Berlin. I had never been out of Sweden before, so I was naturally nervous. I asked Stiller if I would have to travel alone. He laughed reassuringly and said I would go with him and another of the stars, Gerda Lundequist. And what a welcome Berlin gave us! We were wildly applauded and bombarded with flowers when we appeared on the stage at the premiere. It was my first great occasion.

During our stay in Berlin, Stiller negotiated with a com-

Garbo in The Street of Sorrow *(1925)*

50

pany to make a film which was set in Turkey. He had already written most of the scenario, in which I was to play a leading part. And as soon as *Gösta Berling* was successfully launched we all returned to Stockholm to finalise preparations for the new film. A month later I found myself in Constantinople.

Constantinople delighted me. But things soon began to go wrong for the film. My friend Einar Hanson – who was to die so tragically in the United States – and I used to fill in time by wandering about the city, while Stiller tried to get the project going. Nothing came of it. On Christmas Eve, despairing of getting what he wanted, he left for Berlin.

So I was on my own in the big city. It was the first Christmas I had ever spent away from home. Through the windows of the hotel there were none of the familiar winter scenes of Stockholm, just the fantastic city and the beautiful Bosphorus. Hanson, too, stayed in quite a lot, for he was to play the role of a pauper in the film and was letting his beard grow. Everything was so quiet, almost dreamlike. I often think back to that strange Christmas in Constantinople . . .

At last Stiller returned. But with bad news! The group financing the film had gone bankrupt and there was no more money. Everything, the travelling and all the preparatory work, had been in vain. It was a tragedy. Only Einar Hanson seemed to be pleased. He rushed straight off to the nearest barber and got rid of his horrible whiskers!

We all returned very gloomily to Berlin that spring of 1925. But Mauritz Stiller was not down for long. He found me an engagement with the German director, G. W. Pabst in his new picture, *The Street of Sorrow*. The part of Greta was not an easy one, but gradually I gained in confidence. And it helped playing alongside two great artists, Werner Krauss and Asta Neilson.

Unbeknown to me, Mr Louis B. Mayer, one of the vice-presidents of MGM, was travelling through Berlin at this time, and on the recommendation of our friend, Victor Sjöstrom, went to see *Gösta Berling*. He was very impressed and decided that the man who had made it should work for him in Hollywood. So he got in touch with Stiller in Berlin and the two men began negotiating a contract. It was not until afterwards that I learned Stiller had included me in these negotiations and that I was to go along with him as well! But I had complete confidence in his judgment, and was ready to follow wherever he thought was good for me. Besides, what was I to Mr Mayer? Only a young beginner fortunate enough to have the patronage of one of the masters of the European cinema. When I was shown a contract to sign, I immediately asked Stiller for his advice for he was now as much my business manager as my director. I knew very little about being a businesswoman. The contract bound me to MGM for three years. I was to earn $400 a week for the first year, $600 the second, and $750 the third. My working year was to be forty weeks.

As soon as *The Street of Sorrow* was finished, Stiller and I hurried back to Stockholm to prepare for our departure for America. I had a vague idea that strange things lay ahead of me, some which would be beautiful and exciting, others perhaps dark and painful. But I had little idea really what to expect. For me, a young Swedish girl, to be going off to America was an extraordinary adventure. A farewell to the life I had led so far! My mother was as worried about my departure as I was – but we both tried not to show it. When the day of parting came, my mother as well as my sister and brother came to the station. Her eyes were full of tears.

'Don't cry,' I said to her. 'I shall be back in a year! Just twelve months – and they will pass so quickly!'

'Yes,' she said. 'Only a year!'

But actually almost four years were to pass before I was able to return. And then I would never see my sister again.

America

It was in July 1925 that Stiller and I sailed for America. A young girl, virtually unknown, with a contract that I knew could so easily be broken if I failed. All I had was my youth, my enthusiasm for my art, and what some called my beauty – although I had little inkling of that. I gave little thought to any of these. My faith lay in Stiller. And I comforted myself with the thought that even if I did not succeed, I would at least be an eyewitness to his triumph. How full of irony life is!

We departed from Gothenburg on the *Drottningholm*. It was a marvellous voyage. I adore the sea. It gives me such a feeling of the infinite, of eternal life, of liberty. For the first time I felt strangely free. I spent much of my time on deck. I enjoyed hours of complete solitude. I only made one real acquaintance on board, a little boy called Tommy.

I like children, and I became particularly attached to this one. But his parents wouldn't let me see him much after a while because they thought I gave him too many sweets!

We arrived in New York at night. As soon as the Americans on board caught sight of land they gave great shouts of joy. I didn't understand their feelings then – not until four years later when I in my turn saw the coast of Sweden appear through the mist. To return to one's country after being away a long time is something beautiful and uplifting.

New York with all its noise and traffic filled me with unease. We had to stay there three months. And it was fiendishly hot! At last we took the train to California. I was pleased at the idea that I was going to start work. But, alas, it was not to be. The weeks dragged on; for over four months I had nothing to do but wait . . . and wait.

The first plan had been for me to make a picture with Stiller as my director – but things did not work out that way. So instead I was cast in *The Torrent*, under the direction of Monta Bell. To begin with everything seemed strange and somewhat frightening. The vast size of the studio . . . the number of people in it. And as I didn't speak a word of English, I couldn't understand what was being said around me. The work was very hard. I was in the studio from morning till night. At the end of the day I had only one wish – to go home and rest. Sometimes as I lay exhausted on my bed I thought of my family and my country, and I was desperately homesick for them both.

While I was working on *The Torrent* I settled at the Miramar Hotel in Santa Monica. It was an attractive seaside resort and from my window I could look at the sea, the great swell of the Pacific, coming from so far away – and, oh, so free!

A little later I received a piece of news which immediately made me happy. I was to film *The Temptress* with Stiller as my director. At last! We understood each other so well, I was sure I would be more relaxed and a better actress with him. And so we began. Stiller, of course, had his own special way of going about things, and some of these did not please the others on the film. There was a general disagreement and Stiller was unceremoniously removed from the picture. Fred Niblo took his place. We were both in despair, Stiller and I. He did not know where to turn and I did not think I could go on being directed in English. But still I tried – for six months, from morning to night. And if I was not filming there were always dresses to try on – dozens of dresses. I am not a lover of clothes, you see.

It was at this time, too, that I received a most distressing piece of news – my sister, Alva, had died. I felt shattered, sick, heartbroken. But there was nothing else I could do but go on working. I did not miss a day, I was never late. But I grieved for my poor sister. (When, later, I returned to Stockholm, I took the opportunity of seeing again the film, *The Gay Cavalier*, in which we both appeared as extras. It was a very poignant moment to see her alive again beside me up there on the screen.) Nothing seemed to be going right at this time. My sister dead, Stiller suffering endless problems, and in the studios I was being considered awkward, obstinate and even difficult to manage by some people. Yet the truth was that I often could not understand what I was being asked to do!

After finishing *The Temptress*, I was given the script of the next film MGM wanted me to make, *Flesh and the Devil*. I read it and didn't like the part. Another *femme fatale*! It seemed so ridiculous and stupid. Nothing for me to do but give coquettish glances and play sly tricks. It really didn't interest me. Mr Mayer, though, wanted me to begin as soon as possible. But I didn't. I told him I was tired and ill after all the recent dramas, and I could not start anything new until I had had a rest. I also said I did not think the part suited me. But MGM were determined to start work at all costs. I went back to the hotel in Santa Monica to think over the situation. The very next day the newspapers were full of stories. 'Greta Garbo threatens to quit,' they cried. 'She is impossible to direct, says her studio.' And so on. Forty-eight hours later, I could stand it no longer. I decided to go back to work.

I do not know what I would have done in the weeks that followed if I had not had John Gilbert as my co-star in the picture. I had hardly set eyes on him before. But he was marvellous, young, lively, devoted and enthusiastic. He was on the set every morning at nine o'clock. He was so kind to me, so considerate and attentive that I began to feel better – indeed it was through him that I gained my first real insight into the strange world of America. If he had not come into my life at that moment of weariness and despair, I think I should have left America for good and returned to Sweden.

By the time we finished *Flesh and the Devil* I felt much brighter. I was also cheered by seeing Stiller succeed. He was about to make his three great Hollywood pictures at

With Antonio Moreno in The Temptress *(1926)*

54

Paramount, *Confessions of a Woman*, *The Street of Sin* and *Imperial Hotel*, and I could sense that things were getting better. I was happy for him – and that made my own troubles seem lighter.

But they were not over yet. The next script I was offered made me mad all over again. It was yet another vamp role in *Women Love Diamonds*. The very idea appalled me. I did not want to play any more parts of that kind. I seemed to have reached the crossroads of my career in America at that moment. I went back to my hotel and waited to see what would happen. The next morning I received a call from the studio. Would I go in and see some sketches for the new film? I refused. It was the first time I had really put up any firm resistance to the company. The result was not long in coming. I received a letter saying that I had broken my contract by refusing to go to the studio. And, as I had broken my agreement, they saw no reason to pay me. That day saw the start of seven months without work or wages. What could I do? I had few friends in the film world who could influence things. Leave Hollywood? Perhaps I might have done so – but John Gilbert encouraged me to hang on, be patient. The simplest thing would be to draw up a new contract, he said. But I would not take the first step, and nor would MGM. So the days passed, and with them I thought more and more about leaving. Stiller, who was now busy filming for Paramount, could not help me. And John Gilbert's friendship, comforting though it was, did not make things any better for me. I needed the guidance of someone used to these sort of negotiations.

It was at that point I was recommended to go to Mr Harry Edington. I was assured that he would be able to sort out my complicated situation and put everything in order. I met him and for more than a week we had long consultations every day. At length he declared that he was prepared to manage my affairs. He told me I didn't seem to be anywhere near as difficult to manage as some people were claiming! So Mr Edington got in touch with MGM and a few days later I signed a new, five-year contract. It assured me of the kind of income I had never dreamed of before. And, I hoped, a choice of more suitable pictures. Since then, Mr Edington has handled all my affairs, contracts, income, conditions of work. I owe him a real debt of gratitude. He supported me when my affairs were in a parlous state and relieved me of a great burden.

*

The Torrent *(1926)*

Overleaf: A Woman of Affairs *(1929)*

56

Hollywood Life

With my affairs now in better order, I began to join in the gatherings of the 'Swedish Clan' in Hollywood. In particular there was the Sjöstrom family who became very dear to me. Victor Sjöstrom had come to America a year before Stiller and I, and was very good to us. Whenever we met, I couldn't help spoiling his dear little girls.

I also went riding with John Gilbert – but Hollywood, of course, had to link us romantically. Oh, the eternal question of love! Of course I have loved. How could it be otherwise? Love is the beginning and end of all feminine experiences. And how can one express love if one has not experienced it? One thing of which I can assure you is that I *never* thought of marrying John Gilbert. He, no doubt, wished it. But he also knew I was opposed to marriage. We were friends, very dear friends, but no more. Personally, marriage does not interest me. I cannot say that I shall never marry, but so far all I have wished is to live alone . . . and free!

Meanwhile, I had started work again. I made *The Mysterious Lady* with Conrad Nagel, and *Love*, based on the famous novel *Anna Karenina*, again with John Gilbert. The making of that film gave me great pleasure. Anna Karenina was a heroine I had long admired because she seemed so *real*. Neither all good nor all bad, a simple woman, a real woman, a prey to life, love and grief.

Three more films followed. These were *The Divine Woman*, in which I had the pleasure of working under the direction of Victor Sjöstrom, and co-starring a fellow countryman, Lars Hanson. Then *A Woman of Affairs* directed by Clarence Brown, who had become a favourite of mine. John Gilbert starred with me for a third time: we were now a famous 'team'. And the third picture was *Wild Oats* with another Swedish actor, Nils Asther, and Lewis Stone. I liked the film – my role as a child-woman, instinctive and sincere, suited me.

But I could not forget Sweden all this time. Almost four years had gone by since I left, and I was still rather bewildered by all the changes that had taken place since then. Fame and success had certainly come my way, but in myself I had changed, too. If this fame still seemed rather strange, I had gained valuable screen experience and I wanted to go on making progress. The public seemed to like me, although I had gained the reputation of being an enigmatic and mysterious creature. Me, a simple, peaceful and retiring sort of person! I also felt that now I would be able to satisfy all the needs of my family as well as making for myself the sort of life I loved. But the separation from them grieved me, as had the deaths of my sister and, in the second week of November 1928, that of Stiller. They left wounds I knew would never heal.

All these considerations made me decide to spend that Christmas – Christmas 1928 – in Sweden. Christmas, for the Swedish people perhaps more than any other nation, is a family festival, a time for gathering round the hearth. MGM offered no objection to my going home. But I did so want to travel in peace. So I left without telling anyone, using the alias of 'Alice Smith'. I also put on dark glasses and a brown wig. I couldn't help laughing up my sleeve at this subterfuge. And that is how I escaped the reporters who were even on the boat which took me to Sweden! A crowd had heard about my homecoming and gathered at Gothenburg to welcome the ship, and they greeted me enthusiastically. Their cheering, in my own language, sounded wonderful to me.

How pleased I was to be home. I was delighted to think that at last I should be able to have a rest from the rigours of filming. Time passed quickly, though . . . as in a dream. I visited the Swedish film studios at Rasunda and met many old friends. I was cheered, dined and much sought after. But the best time of all was spent at home with my family. Very soon – too soon, in fact – it was time to depart and return to Hollywood. I embarked from Gothenburg on 9 March 1929 and once again savoured the joys of a sea crossing.

The year which followed was a particularly busy one. A major development had occurred in Hollywood which directly affected me. The talking picture had arrived. Already a number of my European friends had gone home because of the 'fearsome microphone'. At that moment I honestly detested the 'talkies'!

My return to work was, though, in another silent picture, my second with Nils Asther, called *The Single Standard*. Most of the action took place at sea which delighted me for as I have said the sea is one of my greatest loves. All the time I was studying English furiously, trying to perfect it, for I could see that however I might feel, the days of the silent film were numbered.

There was to be one more silent picture, *The Kiss*, which I made under the skilful direction of Jacques Feyder, a man whose work I admired. It was actually made *with* sound, though none of us spoke in it. The part I played pleased me enormously because of its complex femininity and subtle irony. It was a film about real life and I tried to play it as well as I possibly could. *The Kiss* was quite a success – but after this there was no going back. A talkie was inevitable.

Despite my initial hostility, I began to take a great interest in this new development, although I felt nervous about having to speak myself. The film chosen for my sound debut was based on a novel by Eugene O'Neil, *Anna Christie*. In it I played the part of a Swedish girl who had recently emigrated to the United States – which was ideal as far as my accent was concerned.

And so with the arrival of sound in my career, my story is up to date. What does the future hold for me? I do not know. Already I have had my share of success as well as tragedy. I have known love, but death has snatched this away from me. I am young, and will try not to be impatient. I shall let the days pass as they will, ready to accept the different and unexpected aspects of life that fate inevitably holds for us.

I am pleased to be able to bring romance and happiness to people tired at the end of their daily work. I am pleased, too, to be able to escape from myself when I live in these different characterisations. And that is why, as long as the cinema will keep me, I shall give my whole heart to portraying these moving shadows on the screen: varied, complex and as fleeting as human joy and sorrow.

GRETA THE BARBER SHOP GIRL

Sally Ekengren

As Greta Garbo has herself mentioned, shortly before her father's death in 1920, and while she was still at school, she had begun to augment the family's income by working in a barber's shop. Although women being employed in such places was by no means uncommon in Sweden, the thought of Greta as a *tvalflicka* (soap lather girl) has naturally intrigued every student of the Garbo legend. But like so many elements of her life, specific details have remained frustratingly elusive. But details there certainly are — for Sally Ekengren, the sister of the proprietor of the barber shop, a man named Arthur Ekengren, has written an account of this period which was published in *Everybody's Magazine* in December 1933. Sally Ekengren worked in her brother's shop on Gotegatan as cashier and supervisor of the soap lather girls. In recording her impressions, Miss Ekengren tells us that even as young Greta worked, her mind was already dreaming of a more glamorous life . . .

Greta Gustafsson – for that was her real name – obtained her first job as junior assistant in the barber's shop my brother and I ran in a busy street in the south of Stockholm, not far from the working-class district in which she was born.

Then she was a tall, strapping, remarkably pretty girl with rosy cheeks, always laughing and full of fun. At first we were a little afraid of her good looks. She soon became the 'draw' of our establishment. Our clients began to increase by leaps and bounds.

The gentlemen of Stockholm decided suddenly that they preferred blondes, if only to slap soap on their chins. The shop was always full in the evenings. Some clients would phone and make special appointments and then, if Greta was not there, find some excuse for postponing them.

She filled the place with her laughter and vitality. Her work began an hour after she had finished school for the day, when she hurried home, changed, snatched a quick meal, and prepared her home lessons. She was quick and vivacious, both in her work and schooling – strict, conscientious, punctual, and eager to learn all we could teach her.

When the shop was more than usually busy she was not afraid to tackle a job she had never done before, whether it was a shave or haircut. No client was ever heard to complain. I believe she could have scalped them, and they would not have protested! I can picture her now, the future Garbo, changing her coat for a white smock in a small cubicle, neatly arranging her hair, tied with a pink silk ribbon, before a piece of mirror.

This cubicle was also her portrait gallery. Its walls were

plastered with postcard photographs of the hero of her young heart, a young and comparatively unknown Danish actor who was then appearing in a small local revue theatre – now Carl Brisson, famous all over Europe.

She must have been his most ardent admirer then. She found his wavy hair and boyish dimples irresistible. She always blew a kiss to his portrait before she skipped into the shop to lather the raspy chin of one of her own devout admirers.

She never tried to conceal her schoolgirl infatuation. One day Brisson was surprised outside the stage-door by feeling a pair of lovely arms around his neck and receiving a smacking kiss on his cheek. It was Greta! He momentarily ruined her romance by telling her coldly to go home to her mother. . . . Later, however, I took her to the theatre where he was appearing with his ballet of 'The Blue Blondines' and singing new songs. She went wild with excitement and completely forgot how people are supposed to behave in a Swedish theatre. She rose to her feet and shouted 'Bravo, Carl!' with all her strength and without the slightest self-consciousness. The audience stared at her almost as much as they did at Brisson.

It was her duty as junior to sweep and tidy the shop when we had finished for the day. This she did as cheerfully as she did everything else, singing merrily to herself all the time Brisson's latest song:

'This is the girl from Stockholm's "malm",
Tall and slender as the desert palm.'

Her wage was about 7s 6d a week, and she usually made as much again in tips.

Greta's grit had been put to the test when her father died. She was fourteen then, and she loved and admired him with all the worship of her young, impulsive heart. He was a working man living with his family in a small flat in a big apartment house in the cheaper part of Stockholm. She was always to be seen with him on Sundays: they used to work together on the allotment garden just outside the city boundary, where they grew potatoes and other vegetables for the frugal family table. This allotment was Greta's favourite haunt in her spare time: there she dug and weeded and helped to make herself the fine healthy girl she was, with a robust beauty which only the open-air life can foster.

Her father's death was a terrible blow to her. Perhaps it set free in her that poignant depth of emotion which has since touched the hearts of film audiences, that capacity to

32 Blekingegatan, an apartment block of flats in Stockholm where Garbo spent her childhood

express suffering with fortitude and courage which has characterised many of her roles. If it did, she was careful not to show it to others at the time. She had a serious problem to face – that of helping to keep the home together now that there was no breadwinner to fend for the family.

Her elder sister, who has since died, and her brother were already in employment. Greta considered it her duty also to contribute and help her mother to make both ends meet. It was then that she discovered our advertisement for a junior. She was already stage-struck, but resolutely, sadly cast aside her dreams of a theatrical career, applied for the job, and got it. But her sacrifice was not in vain. She was to achieve her dream in the fullness of time, after all. The first public 'picture' ever shown of her appeared in the spring catalogue of a big department store, displaying models in millinery. On the strength of that, she was chosen to appear in a small part in an advertising film prepared by the same store, where she subsequently obtained employment.

We missed her very much when she left, but she had finished school, and we realised that her future could never be bounded by our small barber's shop. We wished her the best of luck, and when she walked out of the door for the last time we did not know we were saying goodbye to a woman of genius who was to become a film star of worldwide fame.

Carl
Brisson

MY LITTLE ADMIRER NAMED GRETA

Though he is hardly remembered today, Carl Brisson — who Sally Eken-gren tells us was Greta's youthful 'heart-throb' — was in fact a highly popular singer in Scandinavia and Europe during the 1920s and 1930s: in particular in Britain where his beguiling smile brought him legions of female admirers. A former boxer turned singer, he later became a successful actor on the stage and in films, and also attracted a great deal of publicity because of his many adventures and romances. In the following article, written for the British *Sunday Express* of 1 June, 1930, Brisson reveals the remarkable story of his meeting with young Greta Gustafsson and all about her wide-eyed infatuation with him. . .

Carl Brisson

One of the most romantic episodes of my life stands out very vividly in my memory because its heroine is very well-known to you all. You call her Greta Garbo! I know her as Greta Gustafsson, and as I write the name the familiar face of the screen fades out and dissolves into another face – that of a beautiful child of fourteen whom I knew long ago in Stockholm.

What drew my eyes into the little barber's shop? Well, what draws your eyes to the moving picture screen? A beautiful face. The same face drew mine – the face of a girl named Greta.

I had never spoken to her, or even learned her name, when one bitterly cold evening as I was about to enter the stage door a figure slipped out of the shadow of the wall and touched my arm. It was she! I was surprised. For a girl to speak to me at the stage door was at that time most unusual, but I have become accustomed to it since. I stammered politely, and she held out something towards me with a smile. I took it. It was a bunch of violets. Violets in Stockholm in January! They might almost have been orchids. As I put them in my lapel I tried to smile back, but I think I was more nervous than she was. I stood hatless and silent, and she made little rings with her shoe in the snow.

Then I saw in a flash all the poetry and sincerity and strangeness of the thing that had happened. Here was I, a young actor, and there was a little girl who worked in a shabby barber's shop, standing in the snow in her thin clothes, and giving me violets – violets that must have meant heaven knows what to her in cost at such a season.

A wistful portrait of Garbo in The Story of Gösta Berling *(1924)*

'What made you do this?' I asked. 'What is your name?'
'I love the theatre, and I love your work,' she answered.

71

'I sometimes see you when I have enough money to buy a seat. My name is Greta Gustafsson.'

'Look here, my dear,' I said. 'I will give you a pass for the theatre, and you can come and see me every night if you want to – and sit in a good seat, too.' And I wrote on one of my cards and gave it to her.

She thanked me, and ran away into the darkness of the theatre courtyard. That was my first meeting with Greta Gustafsson.

I spoke to Greta often after that encounter in the snow. She told me that in order to help her mother, who was very poor, she had undertaken to earn a few shillings a week by helping in the barber's shop. The few coppers that she could call her own she saved until she could pay her way into a theatre. The little bunch of violets, withered by the biting frost of Sweden, must have cost her several empty evenings.

You have heard her voice filtered through the works of a talkie loud-speaker. You should have heard, as I did, the first words she ever spoke in a theatre, and the first song she sang. It came about in this way. I had in my show a chorus number in which I asked the audience to join. First the men sang, then the women, then all together. It struck me one day that I might improve the number by pretending to make a single member of the audience sing the refrain alone. At once I thought of little Greta. That night I saw her in her place in the third row, and as I shouted my new line, 'Now, who will sing it alone?' I looked straight at her.

There was an awkward silence. 'Come on, Greta,' I whispered across the orchestra. She hesitated and blushed, but she answered my smile and rose to her feet as the orchestra swung into the chorus. She sang it through alone, and then the rest of the house joined in, and then I sang it alone, then Greta alone, and then everybody again. I was as thrilled as Greta.

The new bit of 'business' was a great success. Greta, who had seen the show many times, already knew the song by heart, and when I, coming down to the footlights, pretended to search the audience for a volunteer to sing solo, she would pipe up with her 'I'll sing!' every night as naturally and spontaneously as I could wish.

The show closed, as shows will. And so I left Stockholm and Greta, perhaps for ever.

*

A plump teenager named Greta Gustafsson

Overleaf: *A young Garbo in love with acting*

At the end of a year I was in Stockholm again, and there, suddenly, I found Greta in the last place I should have looked for her. The barber's shop had changed hands. It was while I was walking through a department of the famous Bergström stores – a sort of Swedish Selfridge's – that I heard a voice I knew, turned round, and saw Greta! She was selling hats. Still the same Greta I had known, with the same frank but somehow wistful look, yet changed in some subtle way. She had matured, half grown up. Her clothes were smarter, and she had acquired the self-possession of the typical shop-girl. I suppose I must nearly have got her the sack, for I went straight up to the counter, and the customers had to wait while we chatted and laughed.

We parted again, and that was the end of Chapter One of the Greta Garbo saga as I saw it. Chapter Two began a year or so later, while I was playing Prince Danilo in *The Merry Widow* revival at Daly's Theatre, London. Maurice Stiller, the great Swedish film genius, the D. W. Griffith of Scandinavia, whose production, *Hotel Imperial*, is one of the classics of the screen, wrote to me and offered me the leading part in the film of *Gösta Berling*. The leading woman, he wrote, was Greta Garbo. That meant no more than a name to me.

I went to Mr James White, with whom I was under contract for *The Merry Widow*, and asked him to let me go. He refused. It was a sad disappointment to me then, but now I am glad, for Hollywood could never have done for me what England has done.

Nearly nine years elapse. I will tell the story of those years elsewhere, but first you must have Chapter Three. It happened only last year. I went to Stockholm. A large crowd met me at the station. A film was taken of my arrival, and I was asked to be present that night at the theatre where the film was shown. It was almost like getting the freedom of a city.

I was standing in the foyer, shaking hands with old friends, meeting leading men and women in the theatrical and film business, some French, some English, some American – it was an international gathering – when through the crowd there broke a young woman. She was stylishly but simply dressed, manicured, coiffured. Her eyebrows – but need I describe to you one with whom you are all familiar? The name of Greta flashed into my mind, but I dismissed it. There could be nothing in common between the little Greta Gustafsson I used to know and this rare beauty. Then as she came straight towards me she smiled, and complete recognition came in a sudden flash. I caught both her hands in mine and cried: 'Why, little Greta, how beautiful you have become. What has happened to you?'

Greta stopped smiling and looked surprised. This was not the greeting she had expected. 'Oh, Carl!' she said, and broke into a laugh. Before I could recover from my astonishment she turned and darted through the crowd into the manager's office.

'So you know Miss Garbo?' said a voice in my ear. The speaker was a celebrated film magnate.

'Good Heavens!' I cried. 'Is she Greta Garbo? Where is she? I must speak to her.' And I in turn dashed through the crowd to the manager's office. What stories of old times and new times we had to tell each other! How we laughed and almost cried! We were brought to earth by the entry of an agitated official, who reminded me that I was expected to present myself before the public. Before we parted it was arranged that we should have supper together after the show. And so we did. After supper we walked mile after mile through the streets of Stockholm, and back and forth under the lights of the famous Strandvegan, still talking and laughing. She had remembered every one of the songs in *Brisson's Blue Blondes*, and she sang them all to me as she walked.

The official programme for the next night called for a banquet at which Greta and I were to be formally introduced. We kept straight faces while this ceremony was solemly performed. Greta sat directly opposite me at table. I was hungry and began to eat at once. After a few moments I noticed that she had not touched her food. She was sitting with her elbows on the table, and her chin resting on her joined hands, looking at me with an expression of melancholy intensity. It was the wistful attitude that you have seen so often on the screen.

'What's up, Greta?' I asked. 'Why don't you eat?'

'Oh, Carl,' she replied in a hollow voice, 'I don't want food; I only want to watch your beautiful hands as you eat.'

I roared with laughter. 'Is that how the girls keep their weight down in Hollywood?' I asked. 'You are not facing the camera now, you know. Save the heavy vamp stuff for Hollywood and let's eat!'

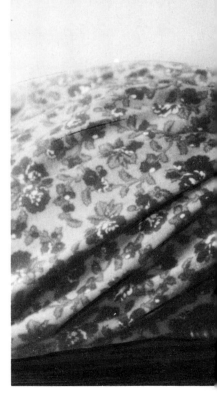

Eugene Nifford # I GAVE GARBO HER FIRST CHANCE ON FILM

As Carl Brisson has recalled, after working in Arthur Ekengren's barber shop, Greta got herself a full time job in July 1920 in one of Stockholm's largest department stores, Paul U. Bergström, popularly known as PUB. Here, on the third floor, she was employed in the millinery department, selling hats. Early the next year she had her first encounter with the camera when she was asked to model some of the store's new hats for their Spring catalogue. The experience heightened Greta's desire to make acting her career, and fellow employees at the store remember that the theatre and cinema were her favourite topics of conversation at this time although, strangely, she made no attempt to join Bergström's amateur dramatic group.

Yet fate was ready to take a hand in her life when a producer of commercial films, Captain Ragnar Ring, spotted her in the store and put her into his advertising film, *How Not To Dress*. Her charm and modest success got her a further engagement in another of Ring's advertising films, *Our Daily Bread*, promoting bakery products. Then when she — quite literally — caught the eye of a producer of film comedies named Erik Petschler she sensed her moment of destiny had arrived. As she has explained, she quit her job in 1922 and made her first full-length film, *Peter the Tramp*, for Petschler. In order to develop her acting skill she also enrolled at the Royal Dramatic Theatre Academy.

Unknown to many students of the Garbo legend, however, Greta had in fact already made a brief appearance in an even earlier feature film called *The Gay Cavalier*, shot in the winter of 1920. This information comes from one of the stars of the picture, Swedish actor Eugene Nifford, who actually provided Greta with this opportunity, and was also on hand to see her introduction to Mauritz Stiller, the man who was ultimately to help her realise her ambition. In the following article written for *Motion Picture Monthly*, in May 1937, Nifford describes Greta's 'debut' and throws some interesting light on a hitherto little-known relationship between her and the Swedish actor, Einar Hanson, who was later to co-star with her in *The Street of Sorrow* and die tragically in Hollywood.

Overleaf: *Lars Hanson and Garbo in* The Story of Gösta Berling *(1924)*

77

It was in December 1920 when I was filming a folk story, *The Gay Cavalier*, on location in the basement of the Palladium Theatre in Stockholm that I chose Greta Gustafsson from a group of extras to be my partner in a dance sequence.

I selected her because I was attracted by her soft, rounded curves. She was plump in those days. As we danced I became fascinated with the thick, long curling lashes fringing the most unusual eyes I have ever seen. Smouldering grey-blue eyes that glowed like moonlight on a blue lake when she looked up at me and said, 'It must be wonderful to be a star.'

In addition to my screen work, I was starring at the Folkstheatre. Einar Hanson, a handsome country lad who had become a great lady's favourite playing juvenile leads at the same theatre, was my roommate. The day he dropped over to our set my casual 'Einar meet Greta' was the beginning of a chain of events that eventually led Garbo to Hollywood.

In the year that followed, Einar left the stage to become the protégé of Director Mauritz Stiller, who was grooming him for screen stardom. We are all familiar with Garbo's progress during this time when she left her job at the barber shop, and later gave up modelling hats at a department store when she won a scholarship to the Royal Dramatic Theatre.

From the first, Greta and Einar were drawn to each other. Although Einar was a reigning favourite, showered with attention and ladies' smiles, he was attracted to this unknown girl of humble birth. But Einar was temperamental and moody. Often as we left the theatre after a performance I have seen him pass Garbo, huddled in a great coat as she stood in the inevitable group that always gathered around the stage door, with only a brief nod in her direction.

At intervals there would be extended periods when he would refuse to see her. These times were usually followed by an explosion from Einar – 'I wish Greta would keep her nose out of my business!' – when he rushed home in preference to listening to a lecture on drinking from Garbo.

It was Einar who brought Garbo to Stiller's attention. I can assure you that by the time Greta had finished making *Gösta Berling Saga*, these two were deeply in love. This annoyed Stiller who maintained that romance interfered with a career. The only discord between Einar and Garbo was Einar's fondness for liquor.

Garbo, Einar, Stiller and myself had just returned from Berlin, disappointed that our plans for filming a picture had fallen through due to the collapse of financial backing, when Stiller received a call from Louis B. Mayer, who was making a tour of Europe. When Mr Mayer invited Stiller to sign a contract to direct pictures for him in Hollywood, Stiller agreed to accept, provided that his protégé, Einar Hanson, was also given a contract. *It was not Garbo upon whom he insisted (as Hollywood seems to believe) but Einar.* However, before Mr Mayer had reached a decision on this proviso, Einar – according to his story to me – came out with the ultimatum that unless Garbo was also given a contract he would not go.

There the matter stood. A triumvirate that could not be broken. For six weeks they dickered back and forth. In the meantime I sold a play and left for New York. A few weeks after my arrival I was at the pier greeting Greta, Einar and Stiller. Greta and Einar – according to Einar – had signed contracts paying each $400 a week.

Those three months were without doubt very happy ones for Garbo and Einar. Together they went on sightseeing excursions. They saw the shows – visited nightclubs. As business called me to Hollywood two weeks before the triumvirate left, I was at the station to welcome them upon their arrival in Los Angeles.

Without doubt the next four months were exceedingly lonely days for Garbo. A stranger in a strange land, she was left to herself day after day. Einar – genial, handsome, generous, was immediately taken up by the smart set of Hollywood. The lad who refused to come to Hollywood without Garbo, now found happier companions. Stiller,

Flesh and the Devil (1927)

80

struggling under the handicap of a foreign tongue and strange American ways, was spending most of his time at the studio. It was during these weeks that Garbo gained the reputation for walking alone. Homesick and alone she filled in the days tramping along the beach or hiking over the hills.

As time went on and Stiller found himself blocked in his attempt to carry out his ideas in Hollywood, he began to stay at home. It was then that Garbo started to drop in to see him. When she received word that her first Hollywood tests were no good, it was to Stiller she turned for advice and consolation.

Einar often salved his conscience for neglecting Garbo by saying, 'I am glad that Stiller and Greta seem to enjoy each other's company.' Take it from me, there never was a romance between those two. A warm affection, yes. An understanding and devotion grew that eventually shaped Garbo's future.

It was during these days that Stiller commenced to coach Garbo seriously. Garbo, who always looked upon

Stiller as the Great Master, was an apt pupil. Among other things he kept continually pounding was that she must diet. 'With your broad shoulders, narrow hips and sleek head, you can take on the glamour of the Egyptian beauties of old,' he would say. 'But you must get slim. Slim as a match.'

It was Stiller who taught Garbo how to walk – the walk that no other actress has been able to imitate. He taught her how to carry her body with the grace of a panther. How to use her hands and her eyes. They discussed life and philosophy. In addition to his technical training, Garbo absorbed Stiller's outlook on life – his attitude toward people and the world.

During this time Stiller told me that Garbo made around twenty-five tests at Metro, none of them good. When the verdict came that she was not considered screen material, it was Stiller who arranged for another test. It was due to his supervision that this test resulted in her being cast in *The Temptress*. From that time on her progress is a familiar story.

Stiller's only satisfaction from his trip to Hollywood was the realisation that his pupil had made good. He told me that in Garbo he saw the reflection of his art.

From that day the great art of Mauritz Stiller has lived in Garbo. That is the secret of her success. Here lies the explanation of her intangible charm. This is the answer to her devotion to the memory of the great director.

By this time Einar had become in great demand in Hollywood. He was earning more money than he had ever earned before. But he was drifting farther and farther away from Garbo and Stiller. As both he and I were prospering, we rented Conrad Nagel's beach home on the Malibu road. To celebrate we gave a dinner, inviting Garbo and Stiller.

It was to be an informal, old-time get-together on the cook's night out. The kind of evening we all loved. Garbo, who disliked dressing, came in her favourite brown tweed suit and low, heavy English walking shoes. Garbo was very gay that evening. She came in calling out her usual greeting to us – 'Tjanare', a slang expression of endearment meaning, 'Hello, my boys'.

We had prepared Swedish meat balls, Garbo's favourite dish. That night she could not seem to get enough of them. Finally, Stiller protested. 'You are eating so many meat balls, Greta,' he frowned, 'that if you do not watch out you will turn into one yourself.' Stiller never saw

Garbo as slender as he wished her to be. If he could see her today I know that he would be satisfied.

During this evening, which was to be the last we four ever were to spend together, everything went smoothly until Einar began to partake too freely of Swedish punch. Garbo, without a word, abruptly got up and left. Stiller went with her.

Soon after the door closed, Clara Bow telephoned, inviting us to join a party in progress at her house. When I declined Einar ran outside, jumped into his high-powered roadster and was off. At three o'clock that morning he was found pinned under his over-turned car in the ditch on Malibu road. He had been dead for more than an hour.

Garbo was stunned. For a week she refused to leave her apartment. It was a terrible shock to Stiller. In a short time he returned to Sweden. A few months later, he, too, was dead. Garbo was left in Hollywood to carry on alone.

Do not these unknown facts of Garbo's life explain her aloofness, her attitude toward life, the secret of her success? Is it not easier to understand why she lives so apart from Hollywood? Why it is that her native land will always be home?

Victor Seastrom THE MAN WHO FOUND GARBO

The young Greta Gustafsson met Mauritz Stiller, the man who was to shape her destiny, in 1923 when she was eighteen. As she has told us, she went to meet the famous film director with some trepidation, and indeed the seeming indifference with which he treated her seemed to justify her worst fears that a screen career was beyond her capabilities. When, however, he telephoned to offer her a job, Greta was beside herself with excitement. Sweden's finest director had offered *her* a part! The relationship between these two (much like that of Svengali and Trilby, some observers have claimed) was, in time, to lead to Hollywood and stardom for Greta, but surprisingly only frustration and an early death for Stiller. Stiller was, however, without doubt, the greatest influence on Greta's life and perhaps the only man she ever truly loved.

Born in Finland in 1883, the son of a Russian Army musician, he had fled to Sweden in his late teens to avoid Russian compulsory military training. Penniless and unknown, he managed to secure a job with a small experimental theatre, and there worked his way up to become director until the company collapsed. Fortunately, he was able to get a job at Svenska Bio (which became Svensk Filmindustri in 1919), where he began to make two- and three-reel pictures, and came under the influence of Victor Sjostrom (more familiarly known as Seastrom), who introduced him to the full-length film and, in particular, the literary works of the popular Swedish novelist, Selma Lagerlöf. From Lagerlöf's books, Stiller was to create two of his finest pictures, *Sir Arne's Treasure* (1919) and *The Story of Gösta Berling* (1924), which presented Garbo to the world at large.

Other than Garbo herself, few people knew Stiller better than his mentor, Victor Seastrom (1879–1960). Seastrom, who has been called 'The Father of the Swedish Film Industry', was an actor who turned director with such success that in 1923 he was lured to America by MGM where he created a string of highly successful pictures including *The Scarlet Letter* and *The Wind*, and directed some of the company's top stars such as John Gilbert, Conrad Veidt and, later, Garbo herself in *The Divine Woman* (1928). He was also responsible for encouraging Louis B. Mayer to see Stiller's work, and when his protégé, complete with the young Greta Garbo, came to Hollywood, he was among the first to help and encourage them. In the following article, written for the Swedish film magazine, *Biografbladlet* in December 1950, he talks with intimate knowledge of the personality, working methods and sad death of his friend, Stiller – 'The Man Who Found Garbo'.

Victor Seastrom with Garbo on the set of The Divine Woman *(1928)*

85

To talk about my work or about myself has always been repulsive to me, and I have made it a principle to follow the good advice of the old proverb: artist, do your work but do not speak. But to say a few words about my friend and companion, Mauritz Stiller, is a different thing.

I am sure that it did not for a moment occur – either to him or to me – that we in those days were doing something that would be remembered and talked about many years later. We happened to enter the job at a lucky time. Lucky for our ambitions. Giving us the opportunity to get out of the prevailing rubbish that at the time was supposed to be 'what the public wants'. We were also lucky to work for a company, Svenska Bio [Swedish Biograph], whose head, Charles Magnusson, was a wise man and who by and by was so wise that he discovered that the best way to handle Stiller and me was not to handle us at all but to leave us alone and let us do what we wanted to do. And what we thought was the right thing to do. Where does a motion-picture director nowadays work under such conditions? There were times when the head office hardly knew more of what we were doing than the title of the picture. And anything called budget-meeting or budget did not exist.

I have often wondered: if Stiller and I were young men now – or relatively young men, at about the same age we were about twenty-five or thirty years ago – I wonder if we would have the same energetic spirit, eager to make something different, something new. One thing is sure: we would never be allowed to make the kind of pictures we wanted to or have the same liberty to make them as we were used to.

Mauritz Stiller with his young discovery

Another thing I sometimes ask myself: would we be

able to compete with the splendid directors of today? I don't think so. Yes, Stiller. He was in a way so 'modern'. He had a great 'show sense' which even nowadays could not fail to impress. He was bold enough to take all sorts of liberties regarding his scripts.

Almost all our pictures were based on novels or on plays, and while I had a certain awe and respect for the author of the book or play – I thought that the author ought to know best the meaning of what he had written – but Stiller was so modern that he made whatever changes in the story that he thought would be of the best effect, regardless of what the author had written. Take, for example, *Gunner Hede's Saga*, based on Selma Lagerlöf's novel *The Legend of a Manor*. The climax of the story winds up with some dramatic scenes of a huge herd of sheep perishing in a snowstorm. This was, of course, a hard nut to crack, especially considering the means we at that time had at our disposal. But as good luck would have it, Stiller happened by chance to see at our lab some shots of a documentary film about reindeer which one of our cameramen had made in Lapland. Stiller was immediately struck by a brilliant idea: change the sheep for reindeer! He stopped the release of the documentary, made use of it to fit his story and added some necessary scenes with close-ups of the picture's young hero. The result: a very effective and entertaining picture. But not very much of Selma Lagerlöf's novel was left in it. It met with a great success, however, and was a splendid motion-picture. And a splendid money-maker. Like all the Lagerlöf films we made.

For a long time Stiller believed that if he could find a suitable female type he would make her a 'star', for whom the world would irresistibly fall. After the luxurious comedy *Erotikon* (made in 1920) he was possessed with this thought. The star should be sophisticated, scornful, superior, but under the shining surface humanely warm and womanly, like Tora Teje. She should also have something of the soulfulness and mysticism encompassed by Mary Johnson in *Sir Arne's Treasure*.

Stiller asked his manuscript assistant on *Erotikon*, the future doctor of philosophy and professor of history Arthur Nordén, to find a suitable name for this visualised international star, and Nordén came to think of the Hungarian king Gábor Bethlen, Gustaf II Adolf's brother-in-law, and suggested the name Mona Gábor. Stiller was delighted and tried the pronunciation in different lan-

88

guages and changes: Gábor, Gabór, Garbo, Gabro. . . .

Later, when the visualised star modestly knocked at Stiller's door, a young, unknown girl, Greta Gustafsson, student at the School of The Royal Dramatic Theatre, summoned by Stiller to see if she was suitable for a part in *The Atonement of Gösta Berling*, he already had the name and a world career clear in his head: Greta Garbo.

Gösta Berling is, I think, a good illustration of Stiller's doctrine of types. For every character, after choosing carefully, he picked out a person who had the appearance for the role. Apart from old experienced actors, most of whom had never appeared in front of a camera, he used amateurs – for example, an internationally well-known photographer, and a famous guitar singer – and semi-amateurs, like the young students Greta Gustafsson (Garbo) and Mona Martensson, and the tiptoe dancer Jenny Hasselqvist.

While looking for someone suitable for the role of Gösta Berling, Stiller thought that the hero from *Across the Rapids* and *Erotikon*, the excellent actor Lars Hanson – later active in Hollywood – was not suitable for this part. Therefore he tested a young Swedish poet – now a theatre critic – and a Russian actor, who could not speak a word of Swedish and had never heard of Gösta Berling, who now has his own theatre in Moscow.

At last Stiller decided to choose the former boxer and revue singer Carl Brisson, now famous in American television programmes for his 'one-man shows' and as the father of Rosalind Russell's husband. His successful career began in a little Stockholm theatre. Stiller tested him in England, where the former boxer was a great success as Danilo in *The Merry Widow*. Stiller certainly would have chosen him had he not suddenly been called to the States.

This is typical of Stiller: as the hero of *The Atonement of Gösta Berling*, loved by all Swedes, the minister who was fired, the romantic Don Juan, the inspired poet, he wanted a former boxer just because he had curly blond hair, a stately figure and a charming personality and was greatly admired by the young girl Greta Gustafsson. I think, though, everyone in Sweden heaved a sigh of relief when, after all, Lars Hanson was chosen.

Overleaf: Garbo was at work on the set of Wild Orchids *when she heard of the death of Mauritz Stiller in November 1928*

I have heard that many people think that Stiller and I cooperated. No, we most certainly did not. I cannot recall that we gave each other advice. I don't think we even read each other's scripts. Perhaps Stiller – he was more inquisitive than I was. We never meddled with each other's

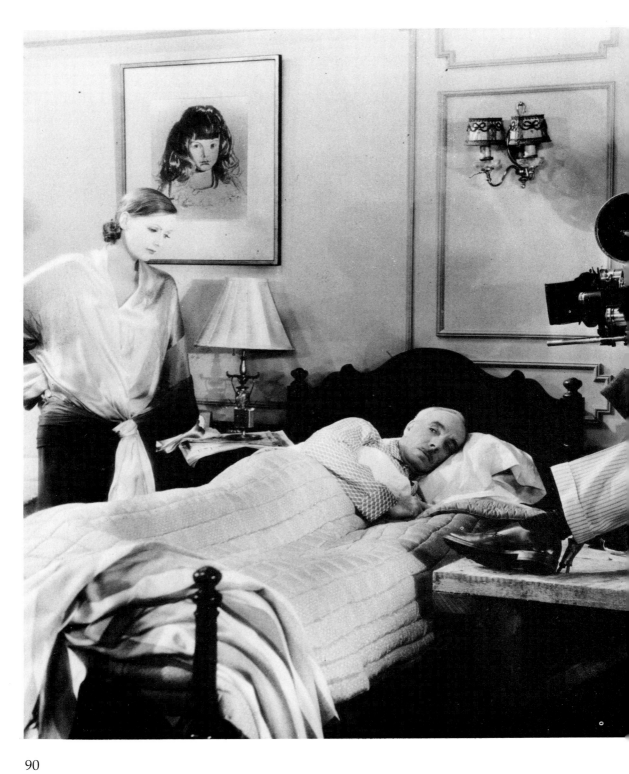

work. Not before we saw the finished picture. We might then give a piece of advice or two about some cutting. But I don't think anyone of us followed the advice. We were both rather stubborn men. We were 'ourselves enough' – to quote Ibsen. In that respect we were of the same sort – but otherwise we were of an entirely different disposition.

We were great, very great friends. And my thoughts go with deep gratitude towards him, thinking of how good and helpful he was to me at a crisis in my life when I needed help. Stiller was four years younger than I. This coming autumn it will be twenty-three years since he died, only forty-five years old. But in spite of all these twenty-three years my memory of him is so vivid, so sharp and strong. Because he was such an extraordinary, outstanding personality. So many different kinds of men were gathered within him. He never shirked or hesitated to call a spade a spade, to tell people straight from the shoulder what he thought. While directing he often lost his temper, he couldn't help it, and it could then happen that he said things that hurt – could hurt badly – and which at the same time were strikingly funny. Although not so funny for the poor victim. But he was quick to make amends, and I don't think anybody was angry with him at heart. And heart – yes, he did have a heart, Stiller. And had it in the right place. I can guarantee it, I am the one to know. And ask any one of the old workers from the Lidingö studio, there are a few of them left and still working at the studios of Svensk Filmindustri in Råsunda outside Stockholm. Real oldtimers. One of them has been working continually for the company since 1912 – for thirty-nine years. And several others follow closely. Talk to any one of these fine fellows about Mauritz Stiller and you will see a light come into their eyes and spread over their faces. And a smile. Smile at the thought of happy memories, happy days, and funny, crazy things he did and said. Let me tell only one that they sometimes talk about. Coming once on the set he found something he didn't like. The foreman tried to argue: 'Well, I thought' – but he was immediately interrupted by Stiller: 'Thought, thought! You shouldn't think – I do the thinking here!' A few days later he again found something wrong. He started to bawl the foreman out but he answered: 'Look, Mr Stiller, you said' – 'I said!' cried Stiller, 'well, can't you think something yourself?'

In spite of our sincere friendship I am not sure I ever knew him profoundly, got deep in under his skin. I don't think anybody did. Still our friendship was a friendship that grew stronger and stronger as the years passed. It reached its top the last day he lived. Sometime late October or beginning of November 1928 my family and I came home from Hollywood for a visit and to let our children have a real Swedish Christmas celebration. It was all a very sad disappointment. When we passed London I heard that Stiller was ill but was not told it was anything serious. Upon my arrival in Stockholm I went immediately to the hospital to see him. The moment I entered the room I saw a man marked by death. What a homecoming. What a reunion. He had left Hollywood a year ago, so happy to go home. He knew now that I was coming and had been expecting me impatiently. He cried like a child when he saw me, and I had to exert myself to the utmost degree to control myself. We had a long talk – he did most of the talking – we even drank champagne in small sherry glasses – it was prescribed by the doctor – and when I left him that day he was cheerful and in good spirits. 'If I live it will be thanks to you,' he said.

Of course, I went to see him every day – an old lady friend from Finland, Prof. Alma Söderhjelm, and I were the only ones he would see – but he became more and more weak. One day when I came home after having been with him for several hours, the nurse at the hospital called me on the phone and told me that Stiller wanted to see me again. He wanted me to come back to him as soon as possible because he had something very important to tell me. I thought he wanted perhaps to talk to me about making his will. He had not made a will – so typical of him. I hurried back to the hospital again and was with him for more than an hour waiting eagerly for what he wanted to tell me. But he only talked about indifferent things. Then the nurse finally came in and said she could not allow me to stay longer, she must ask me to leave. But then Stiller suddenly got desperate. He grabbed my arm in despair and would not let me go. 'No, no,' he cried, 'I haven't told him what I must tell him!' The nurse separated us and pushed me toward the door. I tried to quiet and comfort him, saying that he could tell it to me tomorrow. But he got more and more desperate, his face was wet with tears. And he said, 'I want to tell you a story for a film, it will be a great film, it is about human beings and you are the only one who can do it.' I was so moved I did not know what to say. 'Yes, yes, Moje,' was all I could stammer, 'I will be with you the first thing in the morning and then you will tell me.' I left him crying in the arms of the nurse. There was no morning. Next day he was almost unconscious, he tried to talk but although I put my ear close to his mouth I could not make out what he said. And I don't know if he understood what I said. He only kept on staring at me. A day or two later he passed away.

Greta Garbo

METRO-GOLDWYN-MAYER
PICTURES.

94

Val Lewton GRETA GARBO'S ROAD TO STARDOM

In the opening essay, Greta Garbo herself has spoken about her feelings when she and Mauritz Stiller arrived in America in June 1925 to begin work for MGM. After the peacefulness of Sweden, she found New York, and later Hollywood, almost overwhelming. She was, after all, only nineteen years old and could not speak a word of English. MGM had, though, arranged for the company's New York office to look after the newcomers, and among those who greeted Garbo and Stiller was a young publicity man named Val Lewton. Not long afterwards he followed them to Hollywood where Garbo later embarked on her first MGM film, *The Torrent*. There he was also in a position to observe Garbo's extraordinary rise to fame at first hand. Because of the nature of his job, Lewton was particularly interested in the Garbo 'image' which was to prove such a crucial factor in her appeal, and in the following essay written in January 1932 for *Film Weekly* he gives a fascinating personal view on how this developed. Interestingly, Lewton himself was destined for fame – not as a publicity man, but as a scriptwriter and later a director of some distinction (*The Cat People*, 1942; *I Walked With A Zombie*, 1943, etc.). He also actually worked on one of Garbo's later films as assistant to David O. Selznick, the producer of *Anna Karenina*, in 1935.

A further interesting point about this article are the remarks which the editor of *Film Weekly* addressed to his readers. 'Lewton,' he said, 'has had special opportunities to glean the facts about Garbo. He writes of both her work and her character in a spirit of sober, critical detachment. Greta has always hated the exaggerated "gush" of which she has been made the unwilling subject. It is therefore a tribute to Mr Lewton's perception – as well as to her own intellectual honesty – that it is the only article about herself which has met with her personal approval.'

Val Lewton, publicist turned film director

A biographer of Zola was the first to notice that the names of great personages frequently possess a trumpet sound. He instanced the names of Dumas, Caesar, and Voltaire. Today he might add Greta Garbo's chosen name, which has the same tone and quality as the military call to attention: *ton-ton, ta-ta* – Gre-ta Gar-bo!

But her name, we may reasonably suppose, has had little responsibility for the actress's success. She would have been nearly as successful under her own name of Greta Gustafsson, although this name, as Mauritz Stiller took pains to point out to her at the beginning of her career, labels her too definitely as a Scandinavian, whereas a screen star is an international figure.

It is this universal appeal of Greta which is the real mystery of her career. What is it that so quickly established this gawky, not particularly beautiful young Swedish woman as a world favourite in so short a space of time?

Greta had appeared in only four full-length films, including one that was not universally shown, before she became a star and a leading box-office attraction. It is safe to say that no other player rose so quickly to stardom and then remained so long a favourite. Even now, after six years, there is no wane in her popularity. If anything she is more popular than before.

The Greta Garbo who arrived in America in the late autumn of 1925 was not the Greta Garbo whom screen audiences have admired. The men from the Metro-Goldwyn-Mayer publicity department who met Stiller and Miss Garbo on their arrival in New York were far from being impressed by the actress. Greta Garbo was thinner then than now, nervous, her make-up badly put on, dressed in a cheap ready-made frock, and her hair unbecom-

A shy and rather self-conscious Garbo on her arrival in America

97

ingly arranged in a sort of frizzy bob. Her teeth seemed slightly crooked, and her smile, then, was not a pretty one.

I, myself, was engaged in the New York publicity offices of Metro-Goldwyn-Mayer at this time, and I still remember what a distinct sense of disappointment my first sight of Greta Garbo left on my mind. Later, when publicity pictures of the actress were sent back to New York from Hollywood, everyone at the New York offices who had come in contact with Miss Garbo was astonished to see the vast change which had taken place in less than a month. The girl in the photographs was the Garbo you see on the screen.

What happened during that time? My own surmise is that Greta Garbo had come to the studio and summed up the situation somewhat in this way: Most of the women here are more beautiful than I, and it would be best if I didn't compete with them on their own ground, but rather chose a new style of my own. The frizzed hair, the tight-fitting checked suit, and the other things that had handicapped her were forthwith tossed aside, and the Greta Garbo of the sleek hair, the slow, langorous eyes that look out from beneath sweeping lashes, was substituted for the gawky Garbo we had seen on the pier. Nothing like this had ever before been seen in Hollywood. She could not be classed as either a vampire or an ingenue. And, in being different, Greta Garbo had won her first fight for success in Hollywood. Garbo got her chance within two months of arriving in Hollywood. It was one of the acting plums of the season, the leading role in Blasco Ibáñez' *The Torrent*.

Work started on the picture shortly after Garbo arrived at the studios. It is hard to say who had the most misgivings, the director, Monta Bell, the studio, or Garbo herself. A young Swede, Sven Hugo Borg, was hired to act as Garbo's interpreter, so that the director could give her the full meaning of her role. The interpreter, she says, made her feel awkward and self-conscious. She feared at the time that it might look as if too much of a fuss were being made about her. But it also made her eager to learn English and speak for herself.

At home, after her work at the studio, she studied hard , and before the picture was finished Borg's usefulness as an interpreter had ceased. He remained on the set, but as an actor rather than as an interpreter.

Her remarks in English at this time furnished the studio workers with many a laugh. On one occasion she startled

98

The Street of Sorrow
(1925)

Monta Bell by blithely announcing, 'I am important.' Fearing that his new actress was getting conceited, Bell snapped back, 'What do you mean, important?'

Garbo thought that over for a moment before replying.

'Oh . . . I not mean that! I mean I am *imported* – like sardines!'

From this period in her career may be dated Greta Garbo's abhorrence of certain types of publicity. With true Hollywood zeal the studio press department pounced upon the new 'importation' from Sweden as a means of augmenting their dearly won space in the newspapers. Miss Garbo was browbeaten into posing in all sorts of costumes and with all sorts of celebrities.

Hounded and harried in those early days when her unimportance and her lack of English made her an easy victim of the Hollywood press agentry, it is no wonder that now, when she can say yea or nay, Miss Garbo is so antagonistic to publicity.

MGM-1703

100

Sven-Hugo Borg

HEARTBREAKING DAYS IN HOLLYWOOD

Val Lewton is, surprisingly, rather dismissive of the part played by the young Swede, Sven-Hugo Borg, who was employed as Garbo's interpreter when she first arrived in Hollywood. For, in fact, the star herself was later to pay tribute to Sven for his help and understanding in those early difficult days, in particular helping her overcome the language barrier between herself and the rest of the cast and crew in the studios. Borg has, though, left us his own intimate account of those crucial weeks and months, which was originally published in *Motion Picture Magazine* in May 1932. He was also in a unique position to observe the famous 'love affair' between Garbo and Hollywood's leading romantic star, John Gilbert, 'the screen's perfect lover', which resulted when they were brought together in her third film, *Flesh and the Devil*. At a stroke this partnership put the couple into the headlines of the world's newspapers and placed them among the screen greats, as Adela Rogers St John, the film critic, has observed: 'In the full flowering of their romance, Gilbert and Garbo were added by movie fans to the immortal lovers, Romeo and Juliet, Dante and Beatrice, Antony and Cleopatra. They portrayed love between man and woman as Shakespeare wrote it into his sonnets to the Dark Lady.'

Sven-Hugo Borg, Garbo's interpreter in Hollywood

Borg's long-forgotten essay is perhaps one of the most definitive statements on their legendary romance and throws revealing light on what went on both on the screen and off it. Its reappearance will doubtless be of great interest to all Garbo fans. The essay is also remarkable for the prophetic conclusions Borg draws from his time with Garbo about her future. In introducing his story, he wrote, 'This is *not* a history of Garbo's life. It is merely the attempt of a man who knew her intimately to draw aside the curtain of mystery which has surrounded her strange personality. Many others have written of Garbo's life in Hollywood. Chronologically, they have been correct. I write as one who knew her better, perhaps, even than Stiller, for Stiller was her master and considered her always his protégée.'

was Garbo's interpreter from 1925 to 1929. It was I who taught her her first words of English, and I who guided her through those first hectic months, when, as a frightened, bewildered Swedish girl she lived in the strange and confusing world of Hollywood.

Not only did I act as her interpreter. For more than a year after her arrival in Hollywood she did not have a personal maid. It was I who drove her car, dressed her hair, got her out of difficulties and, in fact, performed every duty of a lady's maid, except, of course, to dress her. Garbo's demands upon me for personal service were so exacting that it was really embarrassing to me, especially when a motion-picture magazine carried the following paragraph:

> The first personal maid Garbo had in this country was a man, and I'm not kidding. Of course, the poor boy did not hire out as a personal maid. He was a Swedish lad named Sven (aren't they all?), and he was employed by the studio to be Garbo's interpreter while she was making her first American picture, *The Torrent*.
> Interpreters are OK, reasoned Garbo, but why let her countryman waste his time? So Sven was commissioned to carry Garbo's shoes from her dressing room to the set (she wore carpet slippers between scenes), and to lug her wraps and make-up box. There was poor Sven, trailing after her, complaining, 'I was hired to be an interpreter, not a lady's maid,' and Garbo, impervious as ever, saying, 'Sven, bring me my make-up mirror,' etc.

A delightful moment on the set of Love *(1927)*

My position as Garbo's interpreter came out of a clear

sky. I had done some dramatic work on the Swedish stage. After several years vagabonding round the world, I decided to stay in Hollywood and try the films. I spoke English well, and had been given an exceptional education, and I felt that I might find a place, as had several of my countrymen, in American films. Arriving in Hollywood, I found it necessary to find some sort of immediate employment to tide me over while breaking into pictures. I was a stranger, so I went to the Swedish Consul, gave him my qualifications and left my application for a position.

On the morning of 13 November 1925, I received a special delivery letter from the Consul, asking me to call at his office. When I did so, he told me that he had been fortunate enough to secure a fine position for me. Of course, I was delighted, but I did not know then what I was letting myself in for.

Metro-Goldwyn-Mayer studios had recently imported a new Swedish actress named Greta Garbo and with her, the great Swedish director, Mauritz Stiller. Since Garbo did not speak English, the studio desired to secure the services of an educated, cultured Swedish gentleman who would act not only as interpreter, but who also would possess the tact and gentleness to guide the girl through the pitfalls of Hollywood life and acquaint her with American customs. The salary was small, but it seemed like an opportunity to bring myself to the notice of studio officials, so I accepted.

I shall never forget my first meeting with Garbo. Strangely enough, Stiller, her discoverer, had not been assigned to direct her. Monta Bell, an American director who spoke no Swedish, was given the job.

A huge garden set had been built on the Metro lot, just to make a test of Garbo. Carpenters, electricians, painters, etc., were still working on the set when I arrived. All was confusion. If I was awed by the magnificence of American movie-making, what of poor Garbo? With features frozen with fear, she stood clinging to Stiller's arm like a frightened child. As I came up, she was saying to Stiller, in Swedish: 'Oh, Mauritz, it is so terrible and confusing! What am I to do? What do all these people talk about?'

I was introduced to both Stiller and Garbo and, with a smile, he said to her. 'Here is a man who has nothing to do except tell you what they talk about; he is to be your interpreter.'

'Oh,' she cried like a child, 'I am so glad!'

With Ricardo Cortez, her co-star in The Torrent *(1926) who hardly spoke a word to her*

It was my duty to translate Mr Bell's orders to Garbo, and as the cameras began to turn for the test, nearly all Metro, it seemed, was gathered to watch the first appearance of the new Star before the camera. I could hear whispers: 'Glorious! Marvellous! A real find!'

'She will be the big Star of the studio,' said Eddie Mannix, a studio executive, to me. 'What do you bet?'

When the test was finished, Mr Bell turned to Garbo and said kindly: 'That will be all, Miss Garbo.' Turning to Tony Gaudio, the cameraman, he added: 'Heavens, Tony, did you notice those eyelashes – nearly an inch long?' She's gorgeous!'

As the cameras ceased to turn, something seemed to leave Garbo, as, I found later, it always did. Drab and colourless when not before the camera, a strange light always seemed to come into her face and a strange power to sway others seemed to shine from her the moment she was being photographed. Perhaps some psychologist can explain this strange circumstance; I cannot. It is so pronounced that even 'grips' (stagehands) notice it, to this day.

I think this is a good place to correct a wrong impression. The story has got about that Metro wanted Stiller, the genius, to direct for them, and that Stiller had refused to sign unless they also gave his protégée, Garbo, a contract. Rather than lose Stiller, so the story goes, Metro signed her for $200 a week, merely as excess baggage, so to speak, not expecting ever to put her on the screen.

That story is false. It was Garbo, not Stiller, whom they wanted. To the credit of Mr Mayer, let it be known that when he saw Garbo on the screen in *Gösta Berling*, he immediately recognised in her that spark which was later to make her the great Star of the films. He doubted whether Stiller could direct pictures which would appeal to American audiences, but Garbo insisted and, *in order to get Garbo, Mayer signed Stiller*. If this were not true, why should the Studio have built a huge garden set, just to give Garbo a test, and why should they not have given Stiller her first picture to direct?

And so Garbo came to America, in company with Stiller and Einar Hanson, later killed in a motor accident near Hollywood. Her salary was $400 a week.

New York awed Garbo. A man named Rolf Laven had been employed as Stiller's secretary, and it was only his influence that induced her to leave her hotel at all. It was Rolf who took her on her first American shopping expedi-

Garbo epitomised – a moment from The Mysterious Lady *(1928)*

tion when Garbo needed shoes. Having been poor all her life, she naturally wanted to go to a cheap store, but Rolf, who had more experience of the value of first impressions – in America especially – took her to a famous Fifth Avenue shop. Garbo wears a size seven shoe and had some difficulty in finding a pair. But when she did, she was delighted with them, until she asked the price.

'But, Rolf,' she wailed, 'twenty-five dollars! (About £5.) That is a hundred *kronen*! Oh, it is terrible!' To this day, Garbo never makes a purchase without first mentally translating dollars into *kronen*, the money of Sweden, which under normal exchange are four to a dollar.

Her next visit was to a famous millinery store. A hat took her eye, but she nearly fainted when she learned that it cost $45.00 (about £9) – 180 *kronen*. 'Take me home, Rolf,' she cried. 'I will not buy from these people who rob me. In Sweden my shoes cost never more than ten *kronen* and my hats, maybe, fifteen.'

En route from New York to Hollywood, Garbo's train stopped for water at a lonely tank on the plains and she decided to get off and stretch her long legs. As the train pulled out, Rolf, by the merest chance, happened to look out of the window. There was Garbo, calmly striding up and down, paying no attention to the departing train. Frantically, Rolf pulled the 'emergency chain', and the train had to back for nearly a mile to the tank, where Garbo sat on a box, smoking. Stiller was angry.

'You must be crazy!' he stormed.

'Not at all,' said Garbo laconically. 'It was great fun.'

By now, having piloted her through *Gösta Berling* and having her under his wing, Stiller's influence upon Garbo had begun to have its effect. There is no question of the uncanny power, a sort of hypnotism, which he exerted over her. Something in him developed and brought out in his protégée that strange halo which is only visible when Garbo is before the camera or on the screen. Confidence in her own future greatness he had also given her, and the independent spirit so prominent in her later Hollywood years was already being made evident.

Many movie stars have been met at the Los Angeles Santa Fé station with a fanfare of trumpets, but no reception ever came nearer to ending in disaster than did that tendered for Garbo. The studio officials had invited a number of prominent Los Angeles Swedish citizens and, as a final touch of grandeur, had engaged a young Swedish nobleman to act as master of ceremonies.

One of the early Hollywood publicity photographs for which – despite her smile – Garbo hated posing

108

Greta Garbo on Strike

Greta Garbo, after being made to pose for hours at a time in running shorts and in other bizarre attires, resolutely went on strike against posing for photos of this description.

109

The baron, it seems, had incurred the enmity of a prominent Swedish artist, a huge man, well over six feet tall, who was also a member of the delegation. 'I've never got even with him,' whispered the big painter to a friend, 'but watch me. I'm going to do it now – right here on this platform!'

The platform was crowded with publicity men, fans and high officials of the Studio, but without another word, the painter pushed his way through the crowd to where stood the baron, resplendent in frock-coat and silk topper. Seeing the huge painter approaching with blood in his eye, the baron lost his dignity and without ceremony took to his heels. It was hound and hare through the startled crowd. The baron was smaller and fleet of foot, and as he ducked through the crowd, the painter after him, people were knocked here and there. And in the midst of it all, the train bearing Garbo arrived!

The baron waited at the steps where Garbo would disembark. His speech had been carefully written out, but when Garbo appeared his hand was shaking so that he could not read it. He began to stutter and stammer, with Garbo looking amazed and frightened on the steps. With a huge lunge the big painter pushed through the crowd. With one big hand he slapped the baron, knocking his silk hat off and upsetting him. With the other, he grasped the startled Garbo by the arm and, lifting her from the train, he said: 'That is all bunk. Welcome to California, Miss Garbo!'

Noticing that all the guests carried packages, Garbo whispered to Rolf: 'And what do they carry, Rolf?'

'Presents,' said Rolf. 'It is customary for them to bring each movie star many expensive presents when they welcome them. Those are for you.'

'Oh, Rolf, that is fine,' giggled Garbo. Then, remembering the prices of the New York shops, she added, 'Oh, I hope it is clothes or something I can use.'

Imagine Garbo's surprise and natural disappointment when, at the reception-room in the Biltmore, the guests began opening the packages without presenting them to her. They contained nothing but a choice assortment of Scotch and Bourbon whisky, which the guests proceeded to drink.

Soon after her arrival in Hollywood, Garbo installed herself in the Miramar Hotel, on the Palisades, above the ocean at Santa Monica. She selected this hotel because of its location, desiring even then the solitude she later went to so much effort to preserve. It being necessary for me to be constantly near her, I moved into the California Hotel, directly across the street. In order to get back and forth between the hotel to the studio, Garbo purchased a small car. It was one of my duties to teach her to drive, and she proved too apt a pupil. As soon as she learned she became a regular speed demon. We would get in the car at the studio and it would be sixty miles an hour until we reached the hotel.

Once she was arrested for driving sixty miles an hour in a ten-mile zone. It was necessary for me to go to the judge in Santa Monica for her. Before doing so, however, I phoned Mr Mayer at the studio and told him about it. He was furious and called up the chief of police. When I went to the station it had been so arranged that if I paid a ten-dollar fine, Garbo would not have to go to gaol. I paid it, but when I returned to the hotel and told Garbo, she frowned. 'Oh, Borg! Ten dollars – that's forty *kronen*! Why didn't you let me go to gaol? I only have six dollars and a half in my purse. Take that, and I will pay the rest later.'

Several times she was arrested for speeding, and always I got her out, once assisted by Louis B. Mayer, by paying a fine. But had she not been a motion-picture actress, no doubt she would have lost her licence, for, quoting Chief of Police Webb, of Santa Monica: 'Of course, we always cater to the picture people, as we want them to be happy with us.'

Unable to speak English and wishing to have her own way, Garbo was quite a trial to her first directors, although they were kind and considerate to her. Not so with Stiller, her master. His profanity, when he became disgusted with Garbo's 'dumbness', would have shocked American ears, could they have understood it. Mr Bell was assigned to direct her in *The Torrent*, her first picture. Stiller was asked to make some tests of her. One request, from the front office, was for a shot of Garbo's legs. As the camera swept the none too beautiful legs of Garbo, Stiller stopped them with a snarl.

'Good lord, Greta!' he roared. 'Cannot we have some sex? Your legs, they are like pipe stems! Look at the legs of this American girl (referring to the script girl). Do like that.' He turned to Rolf and myself with a grimace of disgust and, with an awful Swedish oath, he said: 'The girl is hopeless! She moves about like a cart-horse; no grace of a woman. Make a star of that! Bah!'

And Garbo, as always when Stiller went into one of his

rages, began to sob, which suddenly changed his attitude. He began comforting his 'find' with: 'Aw, but, G-r-e-t-a, don't you know that it is all for your own good?'

One incident, since prophetic in a way, I will tell. It occurred on the garden set built for Garbo's first test. Garbo and I walked over to a piano which was on the set. Garbo sat down and, in that deep, musical voice of hers, sang a single note. Quite in fun, as you will see, she struck with her finger one bass note which so beautifully blended with her own voice that those around stopped and gazed.

'Oh, Borg,' she cried, like a child who had done something wrong, 'it is a real piano, not just a prop!'

And Monta Bell, who was standing near, looked at her and said to me, in English: 'What a voice! If we could only use it!'

Years later, when bill-boards throughout the world blazoned the legend, *Garbo Speaks*, that voice was used with telling effect.

And so, with myself as her interpreter, Garbo began the production of her first American picture, *The Torrent*. Monta Bell was assigned to direct her, and Ricardo Cortez, then at the height of his glory, was to be her leading man. She approached the making of this picture as one approaches an electric chair. Without the guiding hand of Stiller, she was lost.

Stiller's influence had not yet given her sufficient self-confidence to stand alone, and as the day of 'shooting' approached, I was afraid she would collapse. Of course, she was constantly with Stiller, spending every possible moment with him; but she was terrified by the thought that he would not be there when the camera's eye was turned upon her and the picture that would decide her fate began.

'Borg, Borg, do something!' she would plead, wringing her hands. 'Make them let me have Mauritz! Why won't they let me have Mauritz?'

Perhaps my efforts at reproducing Garbo's quotations or actual words seem feeble? I assure you that no person talked less than did Garbo. She had absolutely no small talk and no repartee. If she cracked a joke, it was always sly and subtle, and when you questioned her or tried to draw her out, it was without result. I have actually spent as long as two hours with her without her saying a single word.

At last the day of shooting arrived. I called for her at her apartment quite early, and we drove together to the stu-

112

dio. For once, she wanted me to drive, and as she sat beside me in the little car, she would wring her hands and repeat over and over: 'Oh, Borg! Oh, Borg!'

Cortez had been chosen as the logical successor to Valentino and felt, not unnaturally, rather surprised that he should be called upon to work with this 'dumb' Swede who was nobody. It is therefore hardly surprising that, on the set or off, he paid little attention to Garbo. Cortez is a Spanish name, and Cortez was then supposed to be a full-blooded Spaniard with a romantic background. Someone told Garbo to speak to him in Spanish, as a joke.

'But I do not speak Spanish,' she protested.

'Neither does he,' grinned the joker.

'So?' Garbo lifted those long eyebrows of hers and chuckled. 'Perhaps then, he is really a Swede?'

Although Cortez ignored Garbo, she gave no sign of being conscious of it, except with those long, sideways glances I caught when he was not looking. Never, except in a few close-ups, did he speak to her, and while he was naturally lord of the set, Garbo moved silently into the background. Only when she felt that it was necessary to her part in the picture, did she obtrude herself. Personal slights she could endure calmly, but she resented anything that threatened her work.

The people in the studio did not realise that I was spending hours teaching Garbo English, and they continued as before, to talk in English, thinking she did not understand. 'Hey, Borg, what the blazes is wrong? Get the square-head on the set.' 'Hey, Borg, what's the matter with the big flatfoot?'

Garbo understood many of these slights but never said anything about them. Perhaps, even then, she knew that the day would come when, as queen of the film lot, people would speak in a whisper as she passed. She was profiting by Stiller's influence and her independence grew daily.

Late one evening Monta Bell was trying to catch a fast fading sunset before it died. The scene called for a bomb to be exploded and the first 'take' was a failure, but a piece of the flying bomb had stuck on Garbo's lip. Noticing that she had left the set, Mr Bell called to me: 'Get that woman back here, Borg. If we don't shoot in five minutes we'll have to wait for another sunset.'

I found Garbo offstage, picking the burned fragment from her lip, and delivered Mr Bell's message.

'Tell him not to get excited, Borg,' she said. 'there are plenty of other sunsets coming.'

As I have said, there were times when she could be slyly humorous. One day Mr Bell told me, during the shooting of a scene, to ask her to change her way of doing a certain bit of business. Films were silent in those days, so I called to her, right in the middle of the scene, and told her. Without changing her action, which was supposed to be sad and dramatic, she said in Swedish to me, out of the side of her mouth, but with a twinkle in her eye: 'Tell him to go to blazes for me, Borg.'

I hope no Swedish lip readers saw that picture.

'Ay tank ay go home now' has long been attributed to Garbo as her favourite saying. How often she said it I do not know, but I am sure that I was the first person to hear her use that expression. It was during the first week of shooting on *The Torrent*. Tired, terrified, lost without Stiller, she was ready to drop it all. As she returned to my side after a trying scene, she sank down beside me and said, so low that it was almost a whisper: 'Borg, I think I shall go home now. It isn't worth it, is it?'

A number of humorous things happened on *The Torrent*, due to the fact that Garbo spoke and understood very little English. Doing a very sad and dramatic scene, she was supposed to sit down at a piano, go through the motions of playing, and sing a line or two from the then popular song. 'I want to be happy but I can't be happy till I make you happy, too.' Since it was a close-up and lip movement must be correct, she learned the words, parrot-like, in English, without understanding their meaning. Of course, as she sang the song, she was supposed to turn suddenly from sad to gay. She sat down at the piano, with the camera close up, shooting over the top, face on.

'Ay vant to be happy but ay can't be happy – '. Suddenly everybody laughed, for Garbo – not understanding the words – had continued to look sad and dramatic. She sang so slowly, so sadly, that it was funny to hear those words sung that way. The laughing made her angry until I explained to her, and then she laughed, too.

In spite of Garbo's forebodings and the lack of Stiller, *The Torrent* was a knock-out. The fans hailed a new star, for Garbo's strange appeal held them. Looking back, this was, in my opinion, Garbo's best picture on American soil, including even recent films. Anyhow, it gave the type-hungry fans a new face and Garbo was 'made'. Eager to cash in on this new and exotic personality, Metro rushed her second picture, *The Temptress*, into production, or attempted to. Garbo was overjoyed when it was

114

announced that Stiller would direct. She saw visions of another *Gösta Berling*, a picture that would make her the greatest Star of them all. 'With Mauritz I will show them, Borg,' she would say to me. *'The Torrent*, bah, wait!'

A huge and elaborate Parisian circus ring set was built at a cost of thousands of dollars. Metro intended to spare no expense in its setting for the new jewel. Hundreds of extras were employed and shooting began. Previous to that, Garbo had done two or three dramatic sequences, but this was the real start of the picture. It was a gay scene. Colourful costumes, magnificent trappings. Trained trapeze artistes performed on whirling wheels of fire, and round the ring, mounted on a huge white horse, Garbo rode.

Suddenly I saw a messenger boy push through the crowd. He handed his message to Stiller. I saw Stiller raise his arm brusquely, as with a gesture he stopped the action. Garbo, at his motion, dismounted and came up. Silently he handed her the message and, with a little cry, she sank into a chair, his arm supporting her. The message told her that her sister, her beloved Alva, had died in Sweden. *Until she reads this, Garbo will never know that Stiller held that message twenty-four hours before delivering it to her*! Why he chose that moment, only he knew.

The set was hushed in sympathy as the word spread. For a few moments Garbo was silent, holding her head in her hands, and then she rose to her feet. 'Come, Mauritz, let us go on,' she said, and with a smile she mounted her horse again. The hundreds who saw that have never forgotten it, I assure you. It was the act of a 'real trouper'.

But that was only the first blow. Stiller in his own country had been a god. He wrote the script, supervised production, took care of every detail of the picture. He tried to carry the same method into American studios, but Mr Mayer would have none of it. When Stiller refused to have a supervisor, an assistant director, etc., Mr Mayer became afraid that he had made a mistake, and when *The Temptress* had been in production only one week he removed Stiller.

Stiller was furious, and so was Garbo. She hurried to his side. He stormed and raged, as only he could. He saw the chance to get his revenge through Garbo, his 'find'. 'You are now a great star, Greta,' he told her, in that deep, soothing voice of his, 'and in America great stars do not work for four hundred dollars a week. Tell them that until they give you more money you will not return to work.'

'But, Mauritz,' she protested, terrified, 'they will send me back to Sweden.'

'Not they' – Stiller laughed deep in his chest – 'they will not dare.'

So Garbo disappeared from her studio, and none except Stiller and myself knew where to find her. We arranged a signal that I was to give when I wanted entrance, one long and two short knocks. Detectives were sent out to find her. They trailed me, endeavouring to locate her, but I evaded them. The tension at the studio grew worse. Mr Fred Niblo had been assigned as director to finish *The Temptress*, and when I went into the studio, Mr Mayer asked me to bring her in to confer with him, but I could not move her.

One day she told me that she intended to put the matter in the hands of Milton Cohn, a Hollywood attorney. I informed her that if she did she would only let herself in for huge legal fees. I knew that the thought of wasting her hard-earned money would frighten her. I advised her to see Mr Mayer himself.

'Borg, you are terrible,' was all she would say; 'who are you to know best what to do?'

After a time I was able to induce her to go into the studio to see Mr Mayer. As I knew they would be, things were straightened out, but not before Mr Mayer, who is a patient man, was worn out with her. 'Listen, Borg,' he stormed at me one day, when the last ounce of his patience had been exhausted, 'I want you to get yourself a studio car and go down to Santa Monica and tell her that, to me, she has acted as a simple and ordinary dishwasher would do. Tell her that she can go back where she came from,' adding: 'I'm through!'

As I drove to Miss Garbo's hotel I weighed very carefully in my mind Mr Mayer's words, knowing the drastic consequences which might arise.

Garbo greeted me by: 'Hallo, Borg, come in!' And, with a sly wink: 'Now tell me the bad news.'

Well, quite differently did I convey the given message, as I thought even big men can make mistakes and say things they really don't mean. After much consideration and debating on the part of Miss Garbo, she found it best to follow Mr Mayer's instructions, and reported to the studio. This, I believe, was her first act on her own initiative against Stiller's wishes, and was the end of his influence over her.

Another uncanny thing was the inherent clothes

116

Rare poster of the famous Garbo-Gilbert film Flesh and the Devil *(1927)*

instinct that was hers. Never, until the Metro wardrobe fitted her for *The Torrent*, had she known the feel of really stylish garments, and yet she was as particular and exacting as if she had been born to them. Max Ree, her designer at the time, once said to me: 'It's uncanny! The girl knows absolutely nothing about clothes, at least from experience, and yet her clothes instinct is far better than mine.' And this was the Garbo who used to appear on the streets of Hollywood in an old sweater and trousers!

117

After this interview the gear-shift that combined Miss Garbo with the Metro-Goldwyn-Mayer studios seemed more than ever in need of repair, as gradually the star rose to her zenith.

As we drove down to the beach that afternoon, Miss Garbo stepped on the accelerator to the tune of sixty-five miles per hour. Not a word was exchanged between us. Who knows? Perhaps at that time she fully realised that she was 'licked' and therefore had to take it out on something. After a while she turned to me with an alluring side glance and said: 'Borg, sometimes I could kill you, but you are just a big boy with no sense. Let us get something to eat.'

We stopped at a little Italian café, and enjoyed a wonderful meal together. Garbo's talkative mood passed and she became sad, morose. She drew a deep breath. 'I am so homesick and lonely, Borg. I wish I were home with my poor mother. I wonder if this is all worth it?'

My next is a most astounding revelation about Garbo, one that the world will find hard to believe. A little Italian baby crawled toward us, and Garbo's face became transfigured. With arms outstretched she talked baby talk to him, and when his mother had come and taken him away Garbo said to me: 'Borg, some day I want a little one like that – all my own.'

I have often noticed this inclination of hers towards children. I have seen the mother-hunger on her face too often not to believe what she said. People have, perhaps, placed Garbo on too high a pedestal. They have made it difficult for them to visualise their goddess with normal womanly instincts; nevertheless they are there.

Finding Garbo in a receptive mood, I wanted to get a few things off my chest. 'Now that you have come to your senses,' I told her, 'I want to tell you something. You have felt that Louis B. Mayer is a hard man. One day in his office we talked about you, and this is what he said to me: "Borg, that girl thinks I am a hard, unreasonable man and that I am paying her a salary far below what she is worth. She forgets that it was I who took all the risk. She has acted like a fool and ought to be spanked, but unless she behaves herself she will regret it. I could show you many letters and wires, Borg, from boys and girls who acted silly, as she has, even though it was I who gave them their first opportunity, and every one of them express sorrow and regret for their actions."

'Mr Mayer wants to be fair with you,' I told Garbo, 'and

118

if you have any sense you will listen to him, and some day he will make you a great star.'

'Borg, you are only a big boy, anyhow,' was her usual answer – which she also autographed on the picture she gave me.

Touching briefly upon the mystery of Garbo, I think, perhaps, I was the first to suggest that she capitalise upon the fact that she liked seclusion and privacy. As we lay on the beach at Santa Monica one day I said to her: 'I know you are not acting, Greta, when you hide from people; but, just the same, it is something that fits your personality to be mysterious and secretive. By playing up to it you will kill two birds with one stone; you will get your privacy and also get people talking about you.'

'You think so, Borg?' she said slowly. 'Yes, maybe it is a good idea.'

Again in *The Temptress*, Garbo 'clicked', as they say. Her fame spread. She was the sensation of the studio, and Metro decided that for her next leading man she deserved none other than the 'ace of the lot' – John Gilbert. They were cast as lovers in *Flesh and the Devil*. I believe, with all my heart, that John Gilbert is the only man who ever touched the deep wells of passionate emotion which lie buried deep in the breast of Garbo. She loved John Gilbert, passionately, devotedly – but that love hurt Garbo, and she gave him up.

But let me explain. There was never any thought of marriage between them in Garbo's mind. Not to Gilbert. In his passionate embraces on the set she found the awakening that her own strange nature had hitherto denied her. She was like a child in her happiness, but when she found, as most of us have, that love is no smooth sea, she put it aside, preferring the tranquillity of her own existence to the stormy seas of love.

Stiller was a cynic, a sophisticated man of the world. He often used to say to her: 'Greta, it is good to taste of life, but be careful; do not let it hurt you and destroy you.'

Garbo tried in many ways, at first, to keep her romance with Gilbert hidden from Stiller, who, I shall always believe, knew of it from the first, and chuckled his deep throaty chuckle as he thought of his protégée, his untried little dove, testing her wings on the currents of life. He was too deep, too secretive, too sophisticated to show jealousy, and it was easy to see that he penetrated the subterfuges with which Garbo sought to hide her romance from his eyes.

Overleaf: An idyllic study of Garbo and Gilbert in 1927

The romance of Garbo and Gilbert began with those terrific love scenes in *Flesh and the Devil* in which they were first thrown together. No sooner had those love scenes begun to be filmed than the entire studio was rife with gossip. Even the director Clarence Brown was amazed at the passion, the feeling, that Garbo put into those embraces. I could easily see that Gilbert, even in the mock passion of the screen, had aroused something in Garbo never awakened before. A lesser man than Gilbert would have fallen under that barrage of passion.

As the picture progressed, their performance became stark, bare realism. Clarence Brown was in ecstasy over their work. He caught the significance of it and encouraged it. With arms tightly wound about each other, the two would often fail to hear the word 'Cut', and remain locked in a fond embrace, even after the cameras had ceased grinding, much to the astonishment of everyone on the set. Garbo and Gilbert appeared not to care a whoop that others had discerned their secret.

One day a publicity man said to me: 'Well, Borg, here's copy, and *what* copy! Studio romance flaming and headlines everywhere.'

'And you know what Miss Garbo will think about *that*,' I said.

'Aw, get Americanised,' he snarled. 'All you Swedes are alike. John is a fast worker, and with scenes like that, what could you expect?'

Garbo, when she was not in Gilbert's arms, was distraught. She began to worry about Stiller. 'Oh, what will Mauritz say, Borg?' she would wail. 'What will he think?' But when the script called for another love scene, she forgot her fears.

Until this time, Garbo had not mingled socially with anyone. Now she began to go out, now and then, with Gilbert. She still lived at the Miramar, and Gilbert had a beautiful swimming pool. A special room was prepared for her in Gilbert's house so that she might change her garments undisturbed when she chose to use the pool.

During this period Garbo was another girl. She used to laugh and joke with me and dance like a kid out of school. 'What do you think now, Borg?' she would ask.

'I think it is good for you to mingle with young people and play,' I would tell her.

Often when she had an engagement with Gilbert, she would say to me: ''Borg, you must find a way – you know what I mean – an excuse to give Stiller. I promised to join

Jack this evening.'

'Why not tell Stiller that you are detained at the studio to make retakes?' I would tell her.

'Not so bad, Borg, not so bad,' she would say, tapping her front teeth with her fingernail, as she frowned; 'but what if he finds out?'

'But how is he to find out?' I asked.

'Oh, well,' she would say, throwing herself into the big leather chair which was in her apartment, 'no matter what the consequences, I must keep my word to Jack.'

I would get Stiller on the phone and explain that Greta had been detained at the studios. He would grunt and hang up.

One night Gilbert gave a huge party. Garbo, sulking in her room, refused to come down and join the guests. John, exasperated at last, went up after her. Furiously he pounded at her door. 'Go away like a good boy,' she told him. 'I want to sleep.'

Jack pounded and pounded, but she would not come out. Then, with furious strides, he stalked downstairs, out of doors, and climbed into his car. He roared away, taking the corner on two wheels. A motor cop soon stopped his headlong flight, and Jack was detained. There was a great deal of publicity about it, but Jack was at last released. It looked as if the romance was over, but one day at lunch Garbo, said to me: 'Borg, go down to Jack's dressing-room and talk to him.'

I knew what she meant, for he had not been in touch with her. I went down. Jack had come to the studio in an angry frame of mind. Seeing me, he no doubt anticipated the purpose of my call, for he shouted: 'You go back and tell her she is the cause of the whole damn thing. I never want to see her again!'

I knew, of course, that he referred to his arrest and all his trouble with the police, but I said quietly as I stepped inside the dressing-room: 'If you don't mind, I'll close the door. We have an audience up the street.'

Up the studio street, a group of people had formed, waiting for the fun. Jack glared at me, but I continued: 'If anyone knows the facts, and I do, I consider what you have just said unjust and unfair. You know you didn't mean a word of it. What is the trouble, anyhow?'

'Oh, what's the use discussing it!' Jack strode up and down the floor like a caged animal. Suddenly he sank into a chair and buried his face into his hands. 'But, oh, Borg, I'm awfully sorry, really I am!'

At this moment someone knocked on the door. Like a tiger he sprang to open it. On the step, smiling, stood Garbo. Jack stood back, and, as she entered, I discreetly slipped out and softly closed the door behind me.

Garbo and Gilbert had their brief hour of romance. It is my belief that Jack often pleaded with her to marry him, but I am equally sure that Garbo never, at any time, considered the idea. Stiller's influence, while no longer in complete control as of old, was still on Garbo. He had convinced her that she was a great actress, another Bernhardt or Duse of the screen. He had taught her to taste the sweets of life, but not to let entanglements ruin her career, and she had no intention of so doing, no matter how much she loved Gilbert.

Stiller had, at this time, been assigned to direct pictures at the Paramount studio. He had become even more morose, more brooding than ever. People have said that Stiller died of a broken heart, because of his unrequited love for Garbo, who preferred to remain in the Hollywood which would not have him, rather than return to Sweden with him. But even during her romance with Gilbert, Garbo spent considerable time with Stiller. She would go to his apartment, sit on his lap and smoke the cigarette from his mouth, taking it away from him for a puff with coquettish little giggles. At those times she would talk to Stiller about her problems and he would advise her. If Garbo was ever in love with Stiller, it was a love entirely different from that she gave to Gilbert.

Stiller grieved as he saw Garbo climbing to the heights without him. She was the lovely thing whom his mind had created and who had outgrown her creator. If Stiller died of a broken heart, it was because of this, not because of love for Garbo.

At last Garbo decided the time to end her first and only real love had come. She began to evade Gilbert, and she made no more visits to his swimming pool or to the room set aside for her in his home. Jack brooded. He tried all his powers of persuasion to induce her to renew the old friendship, but Garbo knew that the time had come. Then Jack met Ina Claire. Almost with the suddenness of a bolt from the blue, they were married. Garbo was on location when this news reached her and she took it like the 'real trouper' that she is. On her return to the mainland she voiced her feelings with: 'How nice for them – it is far better, as we cannot have everything,' adding in a mere whisper, 'Garbo must go on alone.'

Previous Page: *Cameraman William Daniels used concealed pencil carbon lights to get this striking shot in* Flesh and the Devil

And so ended Garbo's only romance.

As Garbo's interpreter and general factotum, I, of course, opened much of her fan mail, and was the buffer upon which the efforts of frantic fans, eager to meet her, were expended. A book could be written about the vast volumes of mail she received and the subterfuges which fans used in their attempt to reach her personally. In the hearts of both men and women, Garbo inspired an almost idolatrous worship, so that I was constantly busy protecting her from these inroads against her privacy. But of all those who attempted to see Garbo, one stands out most vividly.

One evening at the Miramar Hotel, I was approached by a young girl. I found that she had ascertained my connection with Garbo, and that she had run away from her home in Milwaukee, determined to see her idol and to be near her. When I informed her that she could not see Garbo, she became hysterical. Frenziedly determined, she took up her stand before the entrance to the hotel, and as Garbo arrived home one afternoon, this girl rushed out and threw herself beneath the wheels of the car, narrowly escaping being crushed. The District Attorney was notified, and the girl, a daughter of a well-known Milwaukee dentist, was immediately returned to her father, who had been frantically seeking her all over the country.

But this episode did not end there. About a year later she was back. During that time she had grown to be a perfect beauty. Boldly she rang the door-bell at Garbo's residence, at 1707 San Vincente Boulevard, and, as the door was opened, she pushed the perplexed maid aside and walked nonchalantly in on Garbo.

Garbo was astonished, and asked the girl: 'What is it that you want?'

'Oh,' was the answer, 'just to talk to you, just to look at you, I guess.'

Garbo was in a predicament difficult to solve by herself, and this was too much for her peaceful, everyday living. She hurried to the phone and called a very close friend (the wife of a certain German writer), and requested her presence, and when she arrived on the scene, she managed to get the trespasser to leave in her company, perhaps more level-headed than ever before.

Withdrawn from the world at large, there were, however, occasions in Garbo's career when she was much fascinated by 'personalities' about the lot. For instance, she had a great admiration for the late 'actor of all faces' –

Lon Chaney. 'Keep on, Garbo,' he once said to her; 'let them write and guess about you, but never let anyone influence you.'

It was not on account of this Chaney advice, given at a moment when the actor was in a philosophical mood, nor was it because of his acting, that Garbo felt such great admiration for him – it was because of his complete withdrawals from social functions, combined with his earnestness, not only to his family and employer, but also to himself.

Their first meeting took place immediately after Garbo's famous studio strike. When Garbo was not present, Lon used to say to me: 'How is the lil' girl today? Tell her to not worry' (thereby referring to her difficulties at the studio), and always there followed many warm-hearted sentences, expressed with utmost sincerity. On the other hand, if he happened to meet with both of us while going to and from a set, then Lon would hurry by without the usual studio greeting of 'How do,' 'You're looking fine,' 'Nice day,' etc. At times like that, Garbo would snuggle close to me and whisper:

'Borg, isn't he nice? Not a sign of that conceit that one sees so much of.'

'Must you not have ego to be a great actor or artist?' was once my comment.

'Yes, one must, that's true,' answered she, 'but not on the surface, as then you become false and will not last, remember.'

It was I who a few days later persuaded them both to have luncheon together, and we selected a table in a far-off corner of that babble-filled studio commissary where Garbo very rarely put her foot.

Garbo was idly listening while Chaney leaned forward trying to converse with her directly, applying himself to a sort of pigeon English. Garmented as he was in a Chinese long coat, and made up as 'Mr Fu', the conversation seemed to have much of an Oriental realism. I know for sure that Garbo did not fully understand all the things he spoke of, but she pretended to, nevertheless, and it was at this luncheon that Chaney said the above-quoted line, while adding: 'Neither let anyone mislead you, Garbo girl – as the boss (meaning Louis B. Mayer) is a mighty level man.'

After this meeting, Garbo and Chaney had many off-set chats and often they sought the company of one another. Never shall I forget the time when Chaney applied a

126

greyish fluid beneath his eyelids to bring forth the realism of a blind person. Garbo stood horror-stricken while watching, and said: 'But L-o-n, is it necessary for you to take such a chance – just think if it would affect your eyes.'

'Not exactly,' answered he – adding as a joke, 'got to do something for the "dough".'

With her always alert mind, she caught a new word and turned to me in her native tongue: 'Quick, Borg, tell me, what is "dough"?'

I explained, and she sighed: 'Oh yes, money – kronen.' On the way back to our set she said again with a sigh: 'That's an artist for you, Borg, a real artist.'

I left Garbo's service with regret. As time went on and she acquired a knowledge of the English language and a better understanding of Hollywood and its customs, she did not require me, and so we parted. Following that, I went into stock at the MGM studio and appeared in many pictures during my stay with them.

I cannot end this story without speaking of my great admiration for Garbo, both as a woman and as an actress. It is my sincere wish that these revelations have helped her millions of fans to understand her to a greater degree, and to know her as a human being with all the rest of humanity's faults and virtues. There is in this Swedish girl, daughter of the common people, that divine spark which has lifted her to a place among the immortals. We lesser mortals shall die and be forgotten, but the name of Garbo will live on.

Pola Negri

I WAS THE FIRST 'EXCLUSIVE' STAR

As Garbo has explained, after the success of *Flesh and the Devil*, MGM proposed that she should film a story called *Women Love Diamonds*. She read the script and found herself cast as another 'bad womens'. Immediately she told the studio she would not make the picture: she wanted a film to develop and expand her career. This time, however, the dispute between star and studio did not last a few hours – but seven months. All this time she held out against the company's mixture of threats and blandishments – not to mention a great deal of criticism in the press over what was seen as her difficult nature and greed for more money – but she won her case. A major factor in resolving this dispute had been Garbo's acquisition of a business manager named Harry Edington, whom she had met through John Gilbert. He took over her business affairs and skilfully negotiated a new contract with MGM worth over £50,000 a year which also allowed her greater freedom in the choice of the roles she played. He also promised to keep the ever-persistent journalists at bay.

Garbo was delighted with Edington. 'He became convinced that I was not as terrible as the papers made me appear,' she told a friend later. 'He sympathised with me and understood that what I wanted was not to make a fuss. I hate fuss. I wanted only the opportunity to make good pictures.' And good pictures she went on to make. Two more vehicles with John Gilbert, *Love* (based on the Tolstoy classic *Anna Karenina*) and *A Woman of Affairs* (from the then notorious best-selling novel, *The Green Hat* by Michael Arlen), *The Divine Woman* in which she was the sole star for the first time in a role based on the life of Sarah Bernhardt, supported by her Swedish friend, Lars Hanson, and directed by Victor Seastrom, and *The Mysterious Lady* in which she played a glamorous Russian spy opposite Conrad Nagel. She was busy on the set on 8 November, 1928, making a fifth picture. *Wild Orchids*, with Nils Asther, when she heard the news of Stiller's death in Sweden. For the second time since she had arrived in Hollywood someone close to her had died – though, like the true professional she had become, she finished the picture without interruption.

Another leading film star who was keenly aware of how deeply Garbo felt this latest loss was Pola Negri who had been a friend of both and was widely known as filmdom's first 'exclusive' star. When the young Greta had first arrived in Hollywood, Negri had been the most famous female star: beginning with her first picture, *Bella Donna*, in 1923, the German-

The exotic Pola Negri

born actress had created a sensation with her series of exotic films which a year later had caused her to be dubbed 'The Reigning Queen of Hollywood'. Pola had developed the 'vamp' image of her predecessor, the legendary Theda Bara, into that of the 'interesting woman', and then in the late 1920s watched this style refined still further by Garbo who was, according to critic Lewis Jacobs, 'the prototype of the ultra-civilised, sleek and slender, knowing and disillusioned, restless and oversexed and neurotic woman who leads her own life'. She had created a new screen type, Lewis went on to explain, '*la divine*, as mysterious and as sovereign as the *femme fatale*, as profoundly pure and as destined to suffer as the young virgin'. Uniquely, too, she appealed to both sexes: men because of her sensuality and women because of her dignity and the depth of her emotion. MGM deliberately promoted the comparison with her predecessor through a series of pin-up photographs captioned, 'Do you think soulful-eyed Greta Garbo resembles Pola Negri? She's supposed to.'

In actual fact there was a closer link, because through the intermediary of Mauritz Stiller the two actresses had met when Garbo was still unknown and they had become firm friends. Young Greta admired the older woman and her talent — an admiration that remained undiminished with the passing years. This friendship continued after Stiller had fallen out with MGM and moved to Paramount where he directed his only great Hollywood success, *Hotel Imperial*, in which Pola Negri herself starred. Both Garbo and Negri had come from similar backgrounds and had to contend with sudden, extraordinary success. Pola Negri chose to lead what she called an 'exclusive' life-style, and had much good advice to offer her friend. In the following article which she wrote for the *New York Herald* in January 1934, Pola explains how she had gone through much the same trials that were afflicting Greta. She also shows great sympathy for the tragic Stiller who had brought Hollywood the girl who was destined to be its greatest star — but at what terrible cost to himself.

An emotional moment from
Wild Orchids *(1929)*

131

In the exotic world of Hollywood I lived a life of my own, a very secluded life according to the judgment of most of the film colony. Instead of acquiring hosts of acquaintances, I gathered around me a few real friends; instead of giving wild parties where everyone could have bathed naked in my swimming pool, or got drunk to their heart's content on contraband liquor, I held artistic soirées where Chaliapin, or any great artist who happened to be in Hollywood, would sing in my house.

The Hollywood of ten years ago was very different from the Hollywood of today, and this attitude of reserve on the part of a newcomer was misunderstood. I was the first star to be called 'exclusive' . . . the catchword which was later to create a new fashion, a new pose for other stars to adopt. Only in my case, it was not a pose, or a publicity stunt; it was a genuine dislike of crowds, a shyness which I have never been able to lose. Because I did not run after the pressmen, pose for my photo to be taken at all hours of the day and night, and rush about Hollywood in a blaze of publicity, I was called a snob, and a 'high-hat'.

I started to grow unpopular and there were even some scathing articles in the papers about 'the star who is too superior to come out into the world'. The director Ernst Lubitsch told me that unless I mixed more with the crowd I should create real ill-feeling and do my career a lot of harm. In a panic, I put on a dreadful forced air of geniality and tried to appear sociable. Lubitsch still remembers how, immediately after receiving his friendly advice, I rushed up to one of the electricians, gave him a resounding slap on the back and said heartily, 'Oh what a nice light you are making.'

Gradually Hollywood realised that my reserve did not

Garbo with her long-time Swedish friend Lars Hanson in The Divine Woman *(1928)*

133

come from snobbishness, but from shyness, and I was allowed to maintain it. I was the pioneer, for after me came a girl who became famous as the shyest star in the whole history of motion pictures, who scarcely went outside her own house and dared to be openly rude to intrusive reporters.

One evening Maurice Stiller, who was then directing my pictures, came to dine at my house. Over the telephone, he asked whether I would allow him to bring a girl who had just come from Sweden, and who had got her first job as an extra at the Metro-Goldwyn-Mayer studio. She was very lonely, for, barring himself, she knew practically no one in Hollywood: her name was Greta Garbo.

My first impression of her when she arrived at my house with Stiller was that she was extraordinarily beautiful, with her smouldering eyes, wistful expression and sweet smile. My next was that she was the dowdiest girl in Hollywood, the town of well-dressed women, where smartness and an air of being well-groomed is almost a religion with even the poorest extra girl.

I found myself wondering whether even Stiller with his genius, his influence, could make a success of someone who so obviously did not know how to make the best of herself. She was very tall, almost like a man with her broad shoulders, and at least ten pounds too heavy for the standards of Hollywood; her hands and feet were large, and she wore a coat and skirt not too well cut, and a felt hat rammed down over her fair hair.

But before the end of the evening, I realised that she had both personality and brains. She was very homesick and unhappy, told me that she hated the studios, the climate, American food, in fact, everything in Hollywood. 'I came here to conquer, and I have to stay here and suffer, I guess,' she would keep saying in her husky voice, and Stiller would look anxiously at her. All through the evening, he never took his eyes off her, and I realised that he, who was one of the greatest directors in Hollywood, and one of the most popular, most sought after men, was passionately in love with this unknown Swede.

As time passed, I got to know Greta well, for she came often to my house. She would sprawl on the rug by the fire, pushing back her long hair from her face, and rail at Hollywood and everything connected with it. She would recount her sufferings at the studio for as long as she could get anyone to listen to her. She seemed quite unable to adapt herself to her surroundings. As she had a great   Love (1927) sense of her own dignity, she was constantly made furious by the supposed humiliations of 'extra' work.

Once she came to me in a perfect fury. 'My God . . . What do you think? . . . Will you believe it? . . . They actually want me to pose with some champion . . . a vulgar prize-fighter.' She was almost incoherent at the insult. 'Some day, some day, you see; I will be as great as Lilian Gish . . . and then I tell them something . . . I tell them all to go to hell.'

I think she would have left Hollywood in those early days, and the screen would have lost one of its most popular stars had it not been for Stiller, who loved her so unselfishly that he would have thrown up his own job, wrecked his career, for her sake.

He believed in her so firmly, this protégée of his, whom he had found working as a manicurist in a barber's shop in Stockholm, and even greater than his belief was his love for her. Stiller was too valuable a director to lose, so knowing that the best way to keep him was to keep Greta,

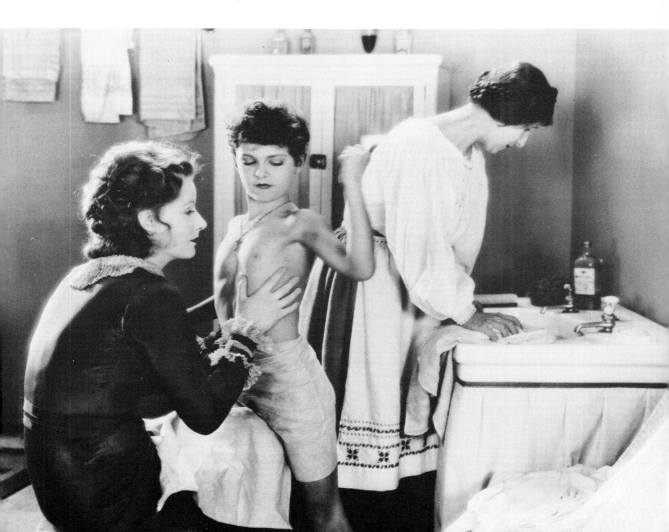

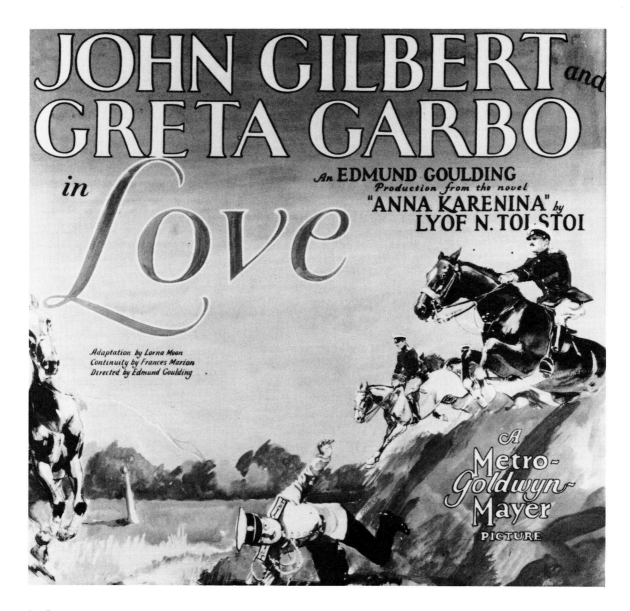

JOHN GILBERT and GRETA GARBO

in

Love

An EDMUND GOULDING
Production from the novel
"ANNA KARENINA" *by*
LYOF N. TOLSTOI

Adaptation by Lorna Moon
Continuity by Frances Marion
Directed by Edmund Goulding

A Metro-Goldwyn-Mayer PICTURE

MGM increased the salary of this obscure extra girl to $200 a week. Time was to prove how Stiller had been justified in his faith in her, and in later years she was to be one of the greatest box-office draws: but at that time she was not worth her $200 salary, and she realised it herself.

She set herself to change her type, reduced her weight, altered the style of her hair, adopted the famous Greta Garbo cut which women all the world over were to copy.

Another rare poster, for Love *(1927)*

When it was done, she laughed over it childishly with me. 'I am quite different now. I see if they like me better.'

One day she said: 'Now I must adopt a pose, something to make them talk about me. You know, I think it would be good to be elusive. I will never be seen in public. All the other stars run after the newspaper men to make them write about them because they are so nice. I will try to make them write about me because I am so rude.'

And all this time Stiller was fighting her battles, giving her all the help and encouragement he could. Then came the day when he lost favour with Metro-Goldwyn-Mayer, because of his passing over other actresses to give parts to Greta, and taking constant close-ups of her. There was a heated discussion at the studio, and Stiller, as proud as he was loyal, resigned. He went over to Paramount, who were only too pleased to secure him. Meanwhile, his championship of Greta had not been in vain. She was given her first big role, and triumphed. She signed a long contract.

Stiller watched the progress of his protégée. Perhaps he fretted that he saw so little of her now . . . that she seemed to have forgotten. Nobody knew what he thought. Behind a calm inscrutability he had a tempestuous soul. Half Russian, half Swede, he had the temperament, the brooding melancholy of both races. But he talked little. In silence he watched the love affair of Greta and John Gilbert, giving no sign. But it broke his heart. I do not think his death was so much the result of illness, as of the lack of will to go on living.

THE DAY THAT GARBO DREADED

Wilhelm Sörensen

Wilhelm Sörensen, Garbo's friend and confidant

Garbo rehearses with a microphone for the first time, with her director, Clarence Brown, on the set of Anna Christie *(1930)*

Overleaf: *'Gimme a visky with chincher ale on the side – and don't be stingy, baby.' Garbo delivers her famous first line of dialogue in* Anna Christie

The death of Stiller and the strain of almost non-stop film-making had exhausted Garbo by the end of 1928, and she decided to take a holiday and go home to Sweden for Christmas. It would be her first return in four years – and in all that time she had not seen anything of her family or her old friends. And so much had happened. She had left her native country an unknown and returned that winter a superstar. Not surprisingly she was greeted by huge crowds, fêted like a Queen, and came finally to appreciate that no matter where she went she was now truly a prisoner of her fame. During her sea voyage home across the Atlantic, Garbo was introduced to another distinguished passenger from Sweden, the young Prince Sigvard, who proved a pleasant and amusing companion. In Stockholm, she met the Prince again, and was also introduced to one of his closest friends, a young man named Wilhelm Sörensen, the son of a wealthy Swedish industrialist.

Not surprisingly, this young man instantly fell under Garbo's glamorous spell, while she, too, was attracted to his fresh good looks and honest manner. So enamoured indeed did Sörensen become that he gave up his law studies and followed Garbo back to Hollywood when she returned the following spring to make *The Single Standard* with Nils Asther, and thereafter for the next two years was hardly ever very far away from her side. She was soon confiding in him, and frequently called upon him for help and advice. 'You must be around me,' she told him, 'but don't ever get sentimental.' (In this aspect of their relationship, Garbo had no cause to worry for it has since transpired that Sörenson was a homosexual.) Sörenson was, in fact, a privileged insider when Garbo celebrated her twenty-fifth birthday in 1930 and made her first talking picture not long afterwards. Both were important, indeed critical, moments in her life. The first demanded that she examine where she wanted the future to lead her. The second that she face the challenge of the talkies that had already defeated a number of well-known silent movie stars – John Gilbert among them. How would she sound? Would her voice shatter the magnificent image she had created, sending her audiences into hoots of laughter? Here Wilhelm Sörenson graphically describes Garbo's introduction to the world of talking pictures in an article he wrote for the British *Sunday Express* of 5 June, 1955.

139

It was her twenty-fifth birthday – and from all Hollywood Garbo had asked *me* to celebrate it with her. Her idea of a celebration was a caviar lunch for two and so we found ourselves at the Ambassador Hotel in Los Angeles. In the restaurant it was Garbo who gave the order.

'How big a portion of caviar?' asked the head waiter.

'Enough!' Garbo replied.

Somewhat taken aback, the head waiter nodded and disappeared. At last we were served with a huge tin of caviar, perched on a block of ice, with illumination coming from underneath. A horde of waiters danced attendance on us, like sycophants at a royal court.

Turning to me, Garbo said in Swedish: 'If only they would let us eat in peace!' None of the waiters understood what she said, but they could not mistake the glowering look in her eyes. All of them moved back a few yards.

'Well, damn it,' Garbo said, 'let's pitch into this caviar. I'll have to pay for the whole tin, anyway, and in this place you want to get your money's worth.' When the waiters approached us again, they were surprised to see the tin almost empty.

We drove back to Beverly Hills so that Greta could change clothes before we went to dinner with Dr Ludwig Berger, the film director. What to wear was always a major problem for her. This did not mean that she had a meagre wardrobe. She had a tremendous number of clothes. But she was a little short of evening clothes.

Digging into one of the mothbags, she finally drew out a green plaited dress. 'The last time I wore this was in Stockholm on New Year's Eve. Since then it's been to the cleaners and must have shrunk.'

It certainly *had* shrunk. The hem was high above the knees. But short skirts were in fashion that year.

At dinner I sat next to Pola Negri, the star of silent films, and fumbled around nervously for suitable topics of conversation. Finally I said something about Prince Mdivani, whose romance and marriage with Pola Negri had been talked about all over the world. 'That's all over now!' she thundered at me. 'You must remember one thing, young man – one always makes mistakes in life.'

'What nonsense are you two talking about?' asked Garbo in her sober voice. And then, turning to me, she said. 'Now Sörenson, that's no concern of yours.' After the party I drove Garbo home and then went back to my place. And that was the end of the twenty-fifth birthday festivities.

Despite her gaiety Garbo was worried about her future in Hollywood. The talkies were establishing a firm footing at this time. Many of her closest friends in the European film colony, such as Conrad Veidt and Emil Jannings, had already made their steamship bookings for Europe. Many foreign stars were extinguished – because they could not speak English. Garbo held out in silent films to the very end. In spite of the talkie revolution her silent films were packing the cinemas. But she would have to face the ordeal of a voice test sooner or later. And the idea filled her with dread.

One day her studio sent a message that they wanted her to take lessons in English elocution. Garbo refused point blank. 'What do I need lessons for? They know how my voice sounds, and I intend to talk English the way I do now!' The problem of her accent could be solved for the time being by casting her in a role where it would fit in naturally. For that reason, *Anna Christie*, by Eugene O'Neill, stood high on the list of proposed stories for her talking debut.

I did not meet Garbo so often during the days before the voice test. Then one day she called to say, 'This is it, Sören! Tomorrow's the day when silent Greta gets a voice.'

On the day of the test she telephoned me again at 2.30 a.m. 'Come over here immediately and drink coffee with me. Step on it!' Dressing in record time, I was over to Beverly Hills within the half-hour. We sat in the living room and talked about trivial matters. Then, before either of us had realised it, the clock had struck six, and a few minutes later the two of us were on the way to the studio.

Suddenly it occurred to me that she must have stage fright, though she didn't betray herself with a word. I did not say anything either but just stared straight ahead. Then I heard a voice from underneath the rug beside me in the car. Instead of a rich, deep timbre, I heard the moving plaint of a little girl: 'Oh, Sören, I feel like an unborn child just now!'

Poor Greta! Young as I was I could feel sympathy for someone whom fate had made a world figure – someone who, at heart, was just a charming and very nervous young girl.

Awaiting Garbo at her dressing room in the studio were Alma, her coloured maid and wardrobe assistant, and Billy, her beauty expert. Both of them adored Garbo and on that morning their faces showed acute apprehension. I almost expected Alma to break into a wailing Negro spiritual, but Garbo would have none of this Doomsday atmosphere. Her manner had again changed, and she was now gay and lighthearted about the whole thing. 'You must go now, Sören,' she told me. 'But please stay in the studio, so we can have lunch together later on.'

Just before noon Garbo called me up to her dressing room, and I was astounded to see the change in her. She was no longer an 'unborn child', but a happy young woman – sure of herself and rid of anxieties. 'Well, it wasn't really so bad,' she said. 'though I became a little scared when I heard my own voice.'

Indeed her first lines in *Anna Christie* are fairly memorable. As a prostitute she walks into a dance hall, sits at one of the bar tables, and calls to the waiter: 'Gimme a whisky! Ginger ale on the side. And don't be stingy, baybee.' Her voice is supposed to sound terribly weary, indifferent, and rasping. I had heard her repeat those lines over and over during rehearsals.

'I almost jumped out of my chair when I heard those lines played back to me,' she said. 'But you should have seen how the others reacted. Alma makes a dramatic gesture with her hand towards her forehead and appeals to the Lord. Billy gets hysterics and runs out. Some of those tough boys on the set start clearing their throats. And the director, Clarence Brown, comes up, gives me a big kiss, and says: "Wonderful Greta!" After that, the sound engineer signals to the mixing room, "OK for sound!"'

OK for sound and for Garbo, he could have added. Everyone present seemed to feel that this was a sensation which would shake the whole film world. In any case the

Previous Page: *Garbo as the spy enticing Gustav von Seyffertitz in* The Mysterious Lady *(1928)*

144

test proved that her voice need not be an obstacle to Garbo's future greatness.

On the day of the premiere people started lining up outside the cinemas long before they opened. A seat at one of the cinemas was secretly reserved for Garbo, but she did not turn up. Instead, she and I went down town together the next morning to see the picture. We entered the cinema unrecognised and sat to one side. Garbo watched the whole film, hardly making any comment, but at times she seemed to be suffering in silence. Perhaps an occasional intonation did not sound quite right to her, and she would have liked to change it. But when we sneaked out just before the end, I got the impression that she felt fairly pleased.

Garbo had entered on a brilliant new career.

John Loder A YEAR IN THE LIFE OF GARBO

Although by 1929 there was an almost impenetrable air of mystery surrounding Garbo — protected considerably by her demand to work on closed sets at the MGM studios and by having moved into a secluded new home at 1027, Chevy Chase Drive, a fashionable street in Beverly Hills — she had evidently taken Pola Negri's advice and built up a small circle of intimate friends. Perhaps not surprisingly, she had chosen mainly Europeans, in particular expatriates like herself including the Swedes Nils Asther and Victor Seastrom, the German stars Emil Jannings and Conrad Veidt, and the English actor John Loder, and his Austrian-born wife. The common denominator between all these people was that they could speak Swedish or German (Garbo's second language) and were dedicated to the art of making quality films. None of them — Garbo in particular — felt the need to play any role save that of being themselves when they were together.

Loder and his wife had first been introduced to Garbo at a party given by Douglas Fairbanks at his home 'Pickfair', and seemingly against all the odds became friends — though not without difficulty as Loder has recalled: 'We often called at her house unexpectedly, just as she called on us. But we didn't always find that her door opened to us. Every so often she would not be at home. Then there would follow days when none of us would hear from her. We couldn't get her on the telephone. No one could find out whether she was working or if she had gone out of town on a vacation. Then all of a sudden she would telephone or appear at the door. She never gave any explanations of where she had been. She went on just as though nothing had happened.' However, during the early part of their friendship, John Loder kept a diary of his meetings with Garbo, a year of which was published in *Film Weekly* on 25 March, 1932. It gives us a fascinating insight into the development of this friendship and a vivid picture of Garbo's — albeit restricted — social life in 1929.

John Loder, Garbo's English actor friend

Overleaf: *Garbo enjoyed sport as much off-set as she did on-set in* **The Kiss** *(1929)*

147

148

January 1929

Have met the Great Garbo! She speaks German and so do I. We got on famously. She is seldom seen in public, and does not enter the parade of the gorgeously gowned. She never speaks 'on the air', nor does she attend premières. 'A waste of time,' she says. 'I prefer my 'ome.' Her entry into a Hollywood café is an event. The shop girls hardly know her. The restaurants and the night clubs rarely see her. Garbo is truly the mystery of Hollywood. She has a dual personality. One, exotic, sensuous, glamorous, lives mainly on the screen. The other, reserved, shy, morose, exists in private. At intervals the two meet, but the intervals are rare.

May 1929

Met Garbo on several recent occasions. Once she paid a surprise visit to the Jannings. Jacques Feyder, the French director, whom she hadn't met, was there. As a rule, if she pays an informal visit and sees strangers she goes home. This time she stayed. She liked Feyder, and they talked of making a picture (*The Kiss*) together.

August 1929

Feyder tells me he has found a boy playing in the Montmartre Café orchestra who has all the Garbo requirements. His name is Lew Ayres. I think he'll get the part.

October 1929

Lew Ayres has been engaged for the Garbo film and is at work. She has taken a great fancy to him. Has been overheard to admire his shirts. He has asked for her autograph.

November 1929

I have renewed acquaintance with a fellow named William Sörenson (a chum of Prince Sigvard). He knew Garbo at Stockholm, and has crossed the water to visit her. She is delighted to see him and has long talks about her home town, relatives, and acquaintances. Sörenson is tall and good-looking, the son of a Swedish box manufacturer. He adores Garbo, and is crazy about pictures. We knew each other in Berlin.

Sörenson is driving Garbo's car. Occasionally she allows him to watch her acting, a very great favour indeed, as she is always hidden behind screens while at work. Sörenson wants to direct. I think Feyder may assist him in his ambitions, probably at Greta's suggestion. Yesterday I met them both at Lubitsch's house. Sörenson told me that they often had long walks together. Greta seems interested in him.

I get on with Garbo famously. She talks and chats quite freely, like a schoolgirl. She even jokes, which is rare. Most of our conversation is carried on in German. *The Kiss* is a great success. Greta is interested in talkies, but hates rehearsals. She thinks the entire future of films lies in the mastery of the speaking technique. Her abhorrence of routine will be a drawback, for laborious rehearsals are, at this stage, almost a necessity.

Sörenson and Garbo came unannounced to my house tonight, having walked all the way from Beverly Hills, a distance of four miles! She was full of high spirits, laughing and talking in a deep, throaty voice. They didn't stay long. In the midst of a conversation she suddenly stood up and said, 'We must go,' and went.

December 1929

Garbo pays occasional visits to a coloured club called 'The Apex', in Los Angeles. It is a garish place of checkered-red tablecloths, and paper roses. Garbo seems to like it, and no wonder, as it is quite the most amusing place in L.A., with lots of 'atmosphere' and fun. The negroes sing blues songs, and there is a really marvellous dance orchestra.

Charles Bickford, working with Garbo in *Anna Christie*, and seemingly very friendly with her, was snubbed by the Swedish girl today when he tried to introduce a friend. She won't meet strangers at any price. Bickford is annoyed. He's an independent, hard-fisted man who curries no favour and talks straight.

Garbo appears and disappears mysteriously. She seems to vanish periodically. Can't be got on the telephone; doesn't appear at the studio; melts into invisibility. Queer bird! Her nearest friends cannot locate her. John Gilbert says that at the height of their friendship she would walk out on him and vanish for hours, sometimes days. There is a rumour that she spends long periods locked in her room reading fan magazines and marking the bits about herself. I hear she sends to the corner drug store for papers before they are due, and is always anxious about any

THE PRIVATE LIFE of
GRETA GARBO
by Her Most Intimate Friend

Free Supplement to this week's FILM PICTORIAL

The Only Authentic Life Story!

Just one of many magazines and booklets published about Garbo during the height of her fame in the Thirties

151

references to herself. She reads, among other British magazines, *Film Weekly*. Often she calls for her papers in person, disguised in dark glasses and a low-brimmed hat. But she cannot escape recognition.

Shopping with Garbo is an experience. How that girl can bargain! Today, buying some blue Chinese satin embroidery, she left the shop *three* times before she would come to terms! As we left she observed: 'I won't be cheated!' She earns a thousand dollars a day, and will argue for quite a long time over a small sum.

Winter 1929–30

I wouldn't call Garbo musical, but she loves the Vitrola. She puts on songs by Sophie Tucker when she wants cheering up. Her favourites are 'Low Down' and 'Oh, What a Man!' Sometimes she plays Swedish records. One, a favourite, is about herself. Two people are supposed to be talking about her rumoured friendship with Prince Sigvard of Sweden. The record ends: 'Be careful, Garbo!' She always laughs at this part.

Xmas 1929–30

Spent Christmas Day with Garbo. She said we were to have a real Yuletide party. We did. Garbo personally bought a large number of decorations, many of them from a ten-cent store. She laughed and joked like a child, till a silly woman, in hysterical admiration, gushed over her. Then Garbo froze into silence and ran out.

'My God!' she said to me in German. 'Can't these people leave me alone!' She quickly got over it and was soon shopping again in another cheap store. We went to Musso-Franks for lunch. It is a cheap restaurant with high stools and a long counter and booths along one side. She ordered a steak, fried potatoes, and beer, and enjoyed herself immensely.

Among miscellaneous dishes Garbo has a preference for pickled fish, Swedish cheese, home-made coffee cake, fish omelettes, roast veal steaks (four inches thick), sponge cake soaked in wine, and a special cake containing chopped almonds dipped in absinthe. Wonder what her fans would think about that!

Garbo isn't pleased with *Anna Christie*, although the studio is delighted with it. Marie Dressler has walked off with nearly all the acting honours. Nevertheless, Greta isn't displaying any jealousy. She sent Marie some gorgeous flowers yesterday. During the showing of the picture

152

Garbo kept moaning to Sörenson: 'Isn't it terrible!' I hear she is very discouraged.

Garbo has visited my new Malibu Beach house with Feyder and Sörenson. She went bathing in the morning and hiked along the shore in the afternoon. She loves the water. In the evening she helped to cook and afterwards to wash up the dishes. A great kid!

Studying Garbo, I come to the conclusion she is a peasant at heart – a peasant with a divine flame. Her dual natures war with one another. She is happy and moody in quick changes. She has no routine, no set plans, is a law unto herself. She cares for nobody, is intolerant of bores, loathes interviewers, and will not be publicly exhibited. She wouldn't cross the hall to greet the Prince of Wales. Clive Brook asked me if I could persuade her to meet the English Prime Minister's son, but I couldn't. She said she wasn't interested.

Garbo is looked on as eccentric, merely because she dresses as it pleases her, and doesn't care two hoots for anybody. She is unaffected by convention or fashion, and lives her own life in her own way. I admire her for it.

At Pickfair she danced with Prince George and with Douglas, but I have rarely seen her dancing with anyone, certainly not at any party where she has been specially invited. She likes to appear unexpected and unannounced and leave when it suits her. She is moody and morose at times, and often stays in her bedroom for days. Her bad periods are sometimes before the start of a new film.

Cecil Beaton

WHY GARBO SHUNS THE WORLD

'Garbo talking is even more magical than Garbo silent!' applauded the critics when *Anna Christie* was released under advertising slogans that proclaimed 'GARBO TALKS!' Where numerous other silent stars had failed, she triumphed magnificently, adding a new dimension to her acting through the introduction of her deep, husky, contralto voice. It was 'sensationally effective' said one critic, while the distinguished playwright, Robert E. Sherwood thought the film conclusively proved Garbo was 'the greatest living actress'. Garbo also made a German language version of *Anna Christie* which Jacques Feyder directed, and this she confided to her circle of friends she thought was 'one of the finest pictures I have ever made'. However, despite the fact that Garbo had spoken on the screen, her continued reclusiveness and refusal to be interviewed only heightened the public curiosity about her. This aloofness – as some saw it – frustrated and even angered some newspapers and magazines who felt that they had helped make her a star and were now being ignored. Reporters as well as celebrities all tried unavailingly to get near her. Writing of her status in Hollywood at this time, biographer Norman Zierold has declared, 'The adoration Garbo aroused bordered on frenzy, those most seriously afflicted were termed Garbo maniacs. She also inspired scepticism, fierce antagonism, and the kind of misunderstandings and misconceptions which continue to this day. Strong-willed and resilient, Garbo survived a harrowing series of critical onslaughts at the very height of her fame . . . their range and intensity are a measure of the extent to which she became, in the thirties, a national obsession.'

As an example of these onslaughts, take Clare Boothe Luce writing in *Vanity Fair* in February 1931 who declared, 'Garbo will be forgotten as a woman in ten years, and as an actress her memory will be dead when Helen Hayes's, Lynn Fontanne's and Katherine Cornell's are beginning to grow greenest. . . . Selfish, shrewd, ignorant, self-absorbed and whimsical, perverse and innocent – she is the perfect realisation of the child left to itself, unhampered and uncontrolled by mature authority. Our generation's loveliest woman is but a phantom upon a silver screen – a shadow with the face of an angel of perdition, as substantial as a mist before the moon, the inarticulate, the bad-tempered, and the ''great'' Garbo.' The columnist Jim Tully put an even more scathing male point-of-view: 'She is broad-shouldered, flat chested, awkward in her movements. Her figure is the seamstress's despair. She has no real beauty, but with

Cecil Beaton, who became one of Garbo's intimate friends

Overleaf: Inspiration
(1931)

155

clever lighting and photographing, she becomes graceful and fascinating on the screen. Garbo is the only woman in the world who has made capital out of anaemia.'

Strong though the protests were which came from Garbo admirers about such attacks, they all pale into insignificance when compared to the outcry that greeted the publication of an article entitled 'Exploding the Garbo Myth' in the April 1931 issue of the popular magazine, *Photoplay*. The piece had been written by Katherine Albert, a former publicist at MGM who, like Val Lewton, had been working for the company when Garbo had first arrived in America. 'Greta Garbo is a bad case of agoraphobia,' she wrote. 'What is more she suffers acutely from anthrophobia. She does fear (and hate) people. . . . She is the most bitter woman in Hollywood. I have seen her come on to her set, making the entrance of a queen, causing the prop men to run with chairs, great directors to dash to her with an inquiry about the state of her health, great executives, fearful lest she not appear at all, mop feverish brows. And I've seen the look in Garbo's eyes, a look of diabolic amusement. ''So they did not care a few years ago whether Garbo lived or died! Now they bow to Garbo. Well, make them bow! Make them bend those rusty knees!'' Oh, Garbo is a straight Case D psychologically.'

When *Photoplay* hit the news-stands of America, it provoked an absolute fury from the 'Garbo-maniacs'. Within a matter of days, the magazine had received over 15,000 letters of complaint, which caused the singularly named editor, James Quirk, to comment in his May issue, 'The reaction to a critical article written by Katherine Albert, who dared to question the artistic dimensions and divinity of Garbo, was the most amazing in the history of this publication.' Nonetheless, he never carried such an outspoken piece about Garbo again. Still, though, the insatiable quest to interview Garbo went on, and many unsuccessful journalists turned their failure into a kind of success by writing articles about her very inaccessibility – none more typical of these than the following piece by the English photographer and film designer, Cecil Beaton.

He, like many others, had hoped to meet the alluring Garbo while he was in Hollywood, and like them made capital out of his failure to do so. He arrived after she had completed *Romance* with Gavin Gordon, and was in the last stages of shooting *Inspiration* in which she played an artist's model with Robert Montgomery. What, though, makes Beaton's particular contribution more interesting than any other is the fact that much later, in 1946, he *did* meet her, a friendship developed, and he actually proposed marriage! Although nothing new came of this proposal, the two remained close friends until 1973 when Beaton published his now-famous Diaries which revealed their affair in the most intimate detail. Like others before – and since – who spoke about her, Garbo instantly dismissed him from her circle. As the critic Gertrude Felbin has written, 'The minute they exploit her in the public prints, as they invariably do, she banishes them from the court of Garbo. If you're Garbo's friend and would remain so, you've got to take the oath of silence.'

As the Beaton Diaries, are, of course, easily available, I have chosen to reprint this earlier item from the English *Empire News* of September 1931, written before the couple had met – and in the light of some of its scathing comments, it is perhaps surprising that they ever did!

Everybody wishes to hear the latest news about The Garbo. So did I when I arrived in Hollywood, but the news is that there is none. In Hollywood, although there is still just as much talk about her as ever, they are resigned that Garbo is never seen or heard. So elusive is she that it is doubtful whether she is even spotted by the doorman at the Metro-Goldwyn studios. Norma Shearer says that it is two years since she last saw Garbo – she came to her dressing-room to borrow some waterproof mascara.

This hiding is a complex with Greta Garbo, and she should be psycho-analysed. Each year the situation becomes worse, and by now she is almost incapable of facing people, and the poor woman suffers tortures when being looked at. Instead of taking lunch in the studio cafeteria (where outsiders are barred), she eats sandwiches up in her dressing-room, quite a meagre dressing-room in comparison with those of other stars. On moving from the lot to her dressing-room she has to screw up her courage, clench her fists, pull up her coat collar and march forth as if to the gallows.

She baulks every ruse of the most ingenious of acquaintances who would introduce some friend; she has even been known to hide in cupboards. All this is no affectation, no stunt. It simply is that she has this fetish – that she is very anaemic, and people exhaust, bore and disturb her.

Mauritz Stiller, who took her to Hollywood, was the one man of whom she was fond and by whom she was stimulated, and she says that now he is dead anyone else is but a poor substitute. In a city where all hair is made albino coloured, where even flowers and petrol are dyed the most vivid colours, where smiles are theatrically arch and affectations rampant, Garbo stands out as being one of the

A typically enigmatic pose from Inspiration *(1931)*

Overleaf: *Garbo with her redoubtable co-star in* Anna Christie, *George F. Marion*

159

few genuine souls. She has made a rigid rule about not seeing people and in no circumstances will she see one in preference to another.

She was ambitious and happy in Sweden and Germany at the beginning of her film career; she was determined to be a star when she reached the film metropolis, but that achievement came quickly, and perhaps she feels she has no greater triumphs in store. Two years ago, when she returned from a holiday to her native Stockholm, she was disappointed and concluded that she might as well make up her mind that she is as happy in Hollywood as she is likely to be anywhere. The sun shines there and she adores the sun, but she is temperamental, feeling that she must fight if she is to secure privacy.

Whenever possible she leaves Hollywood and goes into the desert, where no telephone is likely to distract her. When she has to be near her work, she lives in a furnished house that is hidden behind a twelve-foot wall of thick yews. Here she reads, swims, sunbathes, and plays with her kittens and parrot. She will go for long solitary walks in the old beret and macintosh we all know so well, and occasionally she may even brave the populace, pull up her coat collar, and go to see the puppet show in the old Mexican street in Los Angeles.

But she is in terror of being recognised, and should any enthusiast button-hole her, her evening is ruined. Autograph hunters receive a frank 'No'. She resents people being ingratiating, and mistrusts their being even civil; and beware any young man who attempts to give her a light for her cigarette, for she will pay no attention and light up from her own bricquette.

Hardly a soul in the world is allowed to call her Greta; she refers to herself as Garbo. It is a great privilege of friendship to receive from her a photograph, but only in the case of those half dozen in the world whom she considers her intimates will she append a signature.

She feels that her success is just and deserved, but to her beauty she is completely impervious. Outside the studio she never indulges in maquillage. She does not even use lipstick. She is completely unselfconscious, and reserves the airs and gracious graces for the screen. She is what is known as a tomboy, and likes to become sunburnt, with hair messy and wild.

When asked by the company to dress her coiffure carefully or differently, she will say, 'You would not have me a fussy woman?' She considers her mouth might be

improved, and she would willingly exchange her head for perhaps still more elegant legs – the legs she notices before anything else in other favoured women.

What else makes her melancholy? Well, the poor girl cannot always command sleep; in desperation on such occasions she will read most of the night. If only the pain would go from the back of her neck, if only she had not such a headache! She is nervy to a degree, and smokes one denicotined cigarette after another, and 'goes for' her maid, Alma, in that deep gruff voice of hers.

Though she has seen more of Harry Edington, her manager, than any other person in Hollywood, for she has worked with him ever since she arrived in Hollywood, he is still unable to understand her, has absolutely no influence or control over her. He is still 'Edington' to her, and is continually hauled over the coals. It is he who automatically bears the brunt of her various displeasures; it is he who must listen to her grousing at having to wear the clothes and play the parts she does. She hates long skirts and trains and smart hats.

In many ways Garbo is in a position to, and does, dictate to the directors of her films, but in regard to the parts she plays they are adamant; they know the financial success of Garbo as a vamp. She moans, 'I would give anything if I could only be so enthusiastic to give a good performance that I could hardly wait until the morning when it was time to return to the studio.' To be Oscar Wilde's Salome or L'Aiglon is her ambition, but 'Oh, the grind of these worthless pictures.'

In the studio she has become more and more difficult, and fought bitterly with her director, Mr Clarence Brown, while making the current picture *Inspiration*. She resented the story, was so bored with the humdrum routine that she could hardly bring herself to finish the work. She refused to rehearse with the others; she said her best work was only done instinctively on the spur of the moment. Every day she led Mr Brown up a gum tree; the picture is a moderate effort of everyone concerned save Garbo, who shows herself, in spite of her disdain for the triflings of this middling piece, to have acquired a better talkie technique and to be more fascinating and uncannily alluring than ever.

According to Garbo, life is an unhappy business, and you feel it is all a very sad story. She should enjoy her success so much, for she is conscious of the outside world and reads about it and herself, but she is afraid of the world.

Ripley's
Believe It or Not!

GRETA GARBO

THE MOST PUBLICIZED WOMAN IN THE WORLD, HAS NOT POSED FOR A "PUBLICITY STILL" OR SPOKEN A WORD FOR PUBLICATION IN MORE THAN THREE YEARS!

*Garbo's fame attracts the
attention of the famous Ripley
in 1932*

Once, in the Jack Gilbert days, she was unusually spruced up for some party (in those days she could be taken to parties), and someone remarked that if she always looked so smart she would have the world at her feet, to which she replied, 'Who wants the world at her feet?'

She has lately indulged in no serious whims, partly because she is afraid of the publicity necessarily entailed. Very few people understand her, for she is too simple and unaffected a person to be understood in so complicated, perverse, and artificial a place as Hollywood. And she may do something quite critical one day. She may have one more quarrel with some director and quietly leave the whole caboodle, and after the uproar we should never hear any more of her in America. But she is more likely to pocket the money and continue to play vamp parts in dreary plays that on account of her magnetism are commercial winners.

Piqued at not being able to get 'at' her, at being scorned by her, or out of envy, many people may begin to think of her as a bore and chuckle that Marlene Dietrich is challenging her. Though Dietrich is beautiful and in many ways an even more accomplished actress, there is none but Garbo who possesses the distinctive distinguished quality which inspires people to talk of her unceasingly, to proffer the most amazing theories about her. Garbo in each film conquers all with her strange illusive quality.

If once she becomes the topic of dinner conversation, none other will take its place that evening. The wildest talk. 'She is morbid, unhealthy, a fool, a peasant, a high hat. She is clever, does it all for dramatic contrast; she acts instinctively, everything is planned' – on, on, they gabble. Nobody knows anything. Clarence Brown knows nothing of her save that she is by far and away the best artist he has ever had to work with; that each gesture is right; he believes she does not know why.

Some shout that she is no actress – a beauty, yes. Others cry – a beauty, no; an actress, yes. Meanwhile, Garbo, far away, strokes the parrot's head, rebukes her maid, and lights another denicotined cigarette.

163

164

AN INTIMATE GLIMPSE OF GARBO

Cecil Beaton's claim that Garbo was an enigma to everyone around her, even Clarence Brown, the most regular of her directors – he had, of course, begun with the famous *Flesh and the Devil* and worked on her first talkie, *Anna Christie* – is certainly not true. Brown, a stylish, inventive film-maker who was arguably MGM's best director for almost twenty-five years, came to know Garbo intimately, and though he was anxious not to invade her privacy was quick to rise to her defence. As a movie-maker, Brown's hallmark was his ability to reveal sentiment and emotion in all their varieties on the screen, and this skill has been recognised as playing a major part in the creation of Garbo's enduring legend. Undoubtedly his quiet authority on the set suited the young actress, and he won both her confidence and friendship: two assets he greatly prized. He was ideally suited, too, to introduce Garbo to the complexities of making 'talkies' for he had taken an engineering degree at Tennessee University and understood the techniques of sound recording.

Although automobiles had dominated his youth, he became fascinated with the film business in the 1920s and joined the Peerless Studios in New York where he learned his craft from the great French director, Maurice Tourneur. Later, he switched to MGM and there the highlights of his career were his association with Rudolf Valentino, launching Elizabeth Taylor in *National Velvet*, and making seven of Garbo's best films: *Flesh and the Devil* (1927), *A Woman of Affairs* (1929), *Anna Christie* (1930), *Romance* (1930), *Inspiration* (1931), *Anna Karenina* (1935) and *Conquest* (1937). Not surprisingly, he has become known as 'Garbo's Man Friday'! In this interview given to *Film Weekly*'s columnist Stuart Jackson in London in June 1932, he provides a fascinating insight into the work of the woman of whom he declared simply in 1970: 'That Garbo – for me, she was the best.'

Clarence Brown on the set of **Flesh and the Devil** *with* Louis B. Mayer

Overleaf: *Clarence Brown directing Garbo and Gavin Gordon in* Romance (1930)

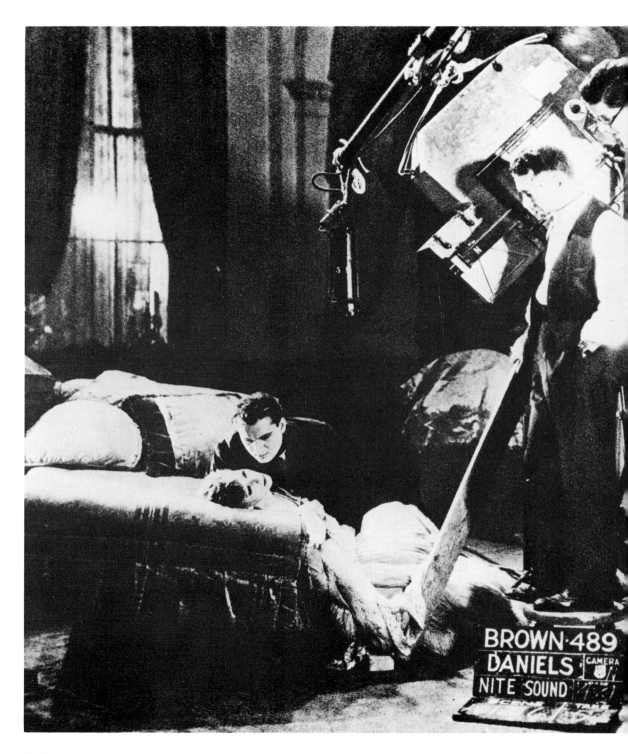

In Room 363 of an expensive London Hotel I found the man who had piloted the famous Greta Garbo through many of her most successful films. When you meet Clarence Brown it is inevitable that the talk should turn to Garbo – and, in his direct way, he will dispel many of the myths about her. I began our conversation by asking him if Greta was a woman with a 'divine spark' – or was it all done by direction?

'Garbo is a business woman,' said Clarence Brown. 'She is in the film business, like the rest of us, for what she can get out of it. That is obvious in the attitude she adopts to all the glamour and glory that her pictures have brought her. She seeks less, and gets more, publicity than anybody. All sorts of silly stories circulate about her.'

'Such as her widely reported threat of "I t'ink I go 'ome"?' I suggested.

'Yes. When Garbo says she "thinks she will go home" we in the studio know that is not a threat. It merely means that she is tired. Anybody is bound to be tired if they are slaving at a picture from nine in the morning until half-past five in the afternoon. When Garbo goes home it is because she feels she is too tired to do justice to the scene she is making. She suggests, quite reasonably, that she will be more equal to it the next day – and we understand perfectly what she means. Greta Garbo is not a strong woman. Her health is much better than it was two years ago, but she has not the physical strength many other players have for the long hours in the studio.'

I reminded him that the newspapers had been printing reports that Garbo intended to turn her back on Hollywood and go home to Sweden.

'She has three new pictures,' he replied, '*Mata Hari, As*

You Desire Me and *Grand Hotel*, two of which can hardly be said to have been released yet. If Garbo decides to go for a vacation to Sweden while those pictures are being shown there is no reason why she should make another picture during that period. If she does go to Sweden, and comes back after six months or so, her return will be like a Second Coming – and will make a great story for the newspaper boys. If Garbo went away, I am sure she would come back. Her strong sense of loyalty would urge her to do that, and it is my theory she would return to MGM who made her what she is.'

Whichever way you tackle him about it, Clarence Brown will tell you that Garbo is not 'difficult'. Nor does she indulge in the 'temperamental' tricks which have been popularly considered a tradition with famous stars. She is just a woman with a job of work to do which she does in a way that is better than anybody else's. Clarence Brown believes that none can compare with her. Mention her alleged 'rivals' and he is somewhat scornful. I happened to link her name with Marlene Dietrich – saying that, whereas the Swedish girl seemed to fascinate her own sex, the German beauty appeared to magnetise the men.

'Anybody who knows them both would not mention Dietrich in the same breath with Garbo,' asserted Clarence Brown, 'Garbo gets her effects from herself. All the director has to do is to lead her gently along, and she will do the rest. But Dietrich is all director. Her work conveys the impressions of a man with a gun – standing over her, forcing her through every action, all the time.'

I told him that any mere man who breathed a word against Garbo in this country would at once have hordes of women eager to tear him to shreds.

'Garbo is not so popular in this country as in other places,' said Clarence Brown, surprisingly. 'Of all the people who see Garbo films I should say that British people were the least enthusiastic.' If that statement does not cause a flutter among Garbo's admirers here I am prepared to sign the pledge!

I then asked Clarence Brown if we could discuss the various films he had made with Garbo, beginning with *Flesh and the Devil*. 'I remember that picture very well,' he said. 'At first she was very distrustful of any director except her Swedish mentor, Mauritz Stiller. And, you see, some people in Hollywood though she was too young at twenty-one to play a middle-aged *femme fatale*. John Gilbert who was Metro's leading star was not enthusiastic about

168

appearing with her, either. But I insisted that she be given the role and once I had introduced Greta and John on the set, I found their mutual fascination added realism to the script. In my opinion, Gilbert has been the only leading man to dominate Garbo.'

Clarence Brown said that right from the outset, no one on the picture ever heard him give directions to Greta Garbo. 'We would go to the side of the stage and discuss the scene in whispers. I was very sympathetic over her fears about visitors to the set. To begin with, the intense lighting prevented the actors from seeing anything beyond the stage. As the film stock improved, the lighting could be dimmed and consequently you could see everything in the studio. When Garbo is actually doing a scene, it is well understood by everybody on the sets that they must avoid meeting her eyes, or she will stumble and stammer . . . and, well . . . just leave off acting. This is no kind of affectation. She cannot help it. She responds very easily to directions, although she will not hesitate to put up a strong argument if she feels differently to her director concerning the way in which she should play a particular scene. Perhaps my success in directing her has been due to my recognition of her as a woman. I realise that the woman in her knows better how the woman character will react to circumstances in the story, than I, a man, can tell her.'

Clarence Brown asserted that he has always been very anxious to preserve Garbo's extraordinary powers of concentration. 'She has something which I have never seen in any other artist,' he said. 'It is something behind the eyes which cannot be seen from behind the camera, but which is there on the film. It is the closest thing I know to the photography of thought.'

I then asked Clarence Brown about his second picture with Greta Garbo and John Gilbert, *A Woman of Affairs*. 'She was much more at ease on this one,' he replied. 'Off camera she felt she was among friends and often did things that were charmingly naive. She has a droll sense of humour, you know. For instance I kept a small projector on the set to run back rushes of the film, and her idea of fun was to run these backwards. She loved the comic effect! It was such a contrast from the role she was portraying on the screen!'

Next I commented on *Anna Christie*, Garbo's first 'talkie'. 'Strangely enough we had very few problems despite what people thought,' Clarence Brown said. 'I was an engineer when I was younger so the sound techniques held no fear for me. The only problem we had was with rehearsing the major scenes. Garbo had always liked to just consult with the director and then do the scene. She said to me, "Clarence, why don't you let me wait until you are ready with the others and then come in."

'I said, "No, Greta. It's not done that way any more." And she got straight on and did it. That film, and *Romance* which followed, gave her screen image the dimension of the tragic heroine which is now her trademark.'

At this point I asked Clarence Brown if he thought Garbo's true metier was tragedy. 'Garbo can suffer and die exquisitely,' he replied. 'I have now directed her in five films, and in three of these I have killed her without any ill effects. In *Flesh and the Devil* she was a suicide; in *A Woman of Affairs*, the same. In *Romance* she died, while in *Inspiration* she was left to her misery. In only one picture have I directed Garbo towards a happy ending. That was in *Anna Christie*, her first, but, in spite of the final fade-out, by no means her best talkie. She certainly can suffer beautifully. And she is incomparable in the art of beautifying illicit love and passion. If you don't think so, just try to name her equal.'

Finally, I asked Clarence Brown who, of course, has been closer to her for as long, if not longer than anyone else, for his candid opinion of Garbo as a woman rather than the mysterious star of the screen. 'When you get her away from people who *will* stand gaping at her as though watching for some visible signs of greatness, Garbo is just a swell girl,' he replied after careful thought. 'She's not talkative, but she is delightfully and entirely feminine. This talk about a masculine complex is just poppycock. I regard Garbo's present relationship to the outside world as one of the greatest tragedies Hollywood has ever known. She wants to enjoy the world as other people enjoy it – unmolested, unobtrusively, spontaneously. But because, if she only set foot on the street in the daylight, she would be mobbed, she must remain in constant hiding. The whole idea may have started as someone's bright joke on the press, but it's no joke for Garbo today.'

Postscript
Though Clarence Brown has rarely given interviews since his retirement in 1952, he did discuss his career at MGM with Scott Eyman of the specialist film magazine, *Velvet Light Trap* in spring 1978. During the

One of Clarence Brown's favourite stills from Romance

course of their conversation, the man who Eyman said has been described as 'Garbo's favourite director', made these further observations about her films – with the added advantage of almost half a century of hindsight.

Flesh and the Devil

'The hardest thing about that story was the ending; we were all stuck for a good one. How do you have the woman die and the two men embrace without making them look like a couple of fairies? It is true that Greta Garbo and John Gilbert were in love, although he was more in love with her than she was with him. Gilbert was a very impetuous, actorish man, very immature, and she had him under her thumb. He was always proposing in front of people, trying to coerce her into accepting. But she always kept him at arm's length.'

Anna Christie

'I won't let anybody knock that picture – I love it. No, I don't think it was a gamble, all you had to do was plaster twenty-four sheets up that said, "arbo Talks" It was more of a gamble for me than for Garbo, because it was my first real talkie. You see when talkies came in, the people in Hollywood saw an opportunity to put all us arrogant, overpaid, sons-of-bitches out of their way. They went to New York and brought out a bunch of theatre directors – there must have been a hundred of them. We learned their business in three weeks, but they couldn't pick up ours. I think that silent pictures were more of an art than talkies ever have been. No matter how you manage it, talkies have dialogue, and dialogue belongs to the stage. Too many people let the dialogue do their thinking for them, do the plot exposition for them, do everything for them. Silents were . . . subtler, I guess.

'In *A Woman of Affairs*, which I made after *Flesh and the Devil*, there's a scene involving an emerald ring that Garbo wears. Gilbert makes a comment about it and she says, " would only take it off for the man I love." Later, they have a love scene on the couch that I shot in close-up. The camera pans from their faces, across her shoulder, down her arm to her hand, just as the ring slips off her finger. Now, once your premise is established, basically via words, the resolution is entirely visual. That sort of thing summarises my ideas about sex, and I think that it's done with a certain amount of imagination and wit.'

Conquest

'That was the last picture I made with Garbo and I enjoyed every minute of it. Charles Boyer was a good actor and a very nice man. Greta's main thing was her shyness; a stranger on a set would upset her. I would never do anything aggressive with Garbo; nobody ever knew what directions I gave her because we'd always go behind a set and talk very quietly about the scene.

'She never actually meant to retire, you know. She was the First, Second, Third and Fourth Star in Europe, and when the War came along, it cut down on that enormous market, which was always what made her pictures so profitable. Metro was cognisant of her appeal, and wouldn't give a theatre a Garbo picture unless they took the whole season of Metro pictures. After the War, the problem became finding the right property for a comeback. About 1950, I suggested a sound remake of *Flesh and the Devil* to Garbo, and she liked the idea. The studio did, too, and I went to work on a script. Two weeks later, during a story conference, I was informed that there'd been some changes; instead of Germany, it was going to take place in South America, so they could use some frozen funds in Argentina. And didn't I think Ava Gardner was a better idea than Garbo? I walked out.

'Garbo was unparalleled. I would take a scene with her and . . . well, it was pretty good, but nothing special. I'd do a couple more takes and couldn't seem to get past that original point. Then I'd go to look at the rushes and it was all there! She didn't act for anybody but the camera. She had something behind her eyes that only the camera could see. Five years ago, I saw her again while we were in Switzerland and she was just the same. The life of the party if she knew you. But let one stranger enter a room and she goes and sits in the corner.'

174

William Daniels GARBO THROUGH THE EYE OF HER CAMERAMAN

Another man in a specially privileged position to observe Garbo at work was William Daniels, an MGM cameraman who was assigned to her first picture, *The Torrent* in 1926, and in all photographed twenty of her films right through to *Ninotchka* in 1939. Daniels was a big, quietly spoken but very direct man, extremely proficient at his craft and with an absolute mastery of lighting. Many of the most famous scenes in which Garbo appeared owe much to his clever variations of texture and shade as well as his occasional use of concealed lighting. Like Clarence Brown, William Daniels enjoyed a friendship with Garbo based on mutual respect, and similarly has been reluctant to discuss her except in the context of her work. More than one film writer has claimed that he had a rapport with Garbo that was probably closer and more long-lasting than any other film maker she worked with.

In 1947, after it was becoming increasingly evident that she might never appear before a film camera again, Daniels wrote this short essay for *Film Monthly*. In it he also helps lay to rest once and for all the myth that Garbo on the set was difficult, often bad-tempered and treated those around her with an arrogance that bordered on contempt. Such were the stories that many newspapers and magazines of the time delighted in carrying. Here Daniels reveals her to have been anything but the gloomy figure she often appeared to be on the screen: instead a high-spirited girl with a sense of humour, popular with fellow actors and technicians alike.

William Daniels, who photographed twenty of Garbo's films

175

When I first arrived at Metro after several years at Universal Pictures where I had been Erich von Stroheim's cameraman, I was asked by Louis B. Mayer to make a special study of Garbo's face and body. He said to me, 'I am a salesman, and part of my job is selling portraits of beautiful women – so it's up to you to give me those portraits.' So I studied the young actress both on the set and off, and the more I looked the more I realised she would be best in close-ups or long shots. She was indifferent in the intermediate range and at her most unattractive when in repose. I also saw that she looked better seated or lying down, even reclining. This was most fortunate when several of her leading men proved to be shorter than she was!

I soon realised that she does things not so much by gestures or postures, but by little things in her eyes. That is why she is superb in the close-ups. She is good in the long-shots because she has such a lovely walk. In fact, she almost runs; the most beautiful walk you ever saw – almost like floating through the air. She walked all the time. She was never still. Between scenes she invariably started walking around the studio and when the scene was ready she might be a mile away, pacing up and down or peeking into other sets, unnoticed.

By giving special attention to lighting, I found I could give added emphasis to those fine features of hers, and in one scene in *Flesh and the Devil*, I had John Gilbert holding two tiny pencil carbons concealed in the palm of his hand as he lit a cigarette. This threw her face into the most striking relief when I made a close-up.

Garbo naturally dominated any picture she was in, but she never did it deliberately. She neither strutted nor posed. She showed herself to be a woman of extreme simplicity, on or off the screen. Another characteristic of hers was that she never demanded favours when in front of the camera. If a scene belonged to another actor in the cast, he or she got everything they deserved, and always with her full co-operation. I have even seen her turn her back to the camera and remain obscurely in the background to give the other actor his opportunity on the screen.

I am happy to say that Garbo and I struck up a friendship right from the start. But I did not actually teach her to speak English as some reporters have written. We used to talk a lot and I would correct her on certain things. We understood each other, and talked about what we both knew – movie talk. I should also like to correct another false impression that working on a Garbo picture was always gloomy. It is true that she liked to know exactly who was on her technical crew, and then the reason why if any changes were made among these men. The crews she worked with adored her. She called the electricians and prop men by their first names, and she was always giving presents to people. One of my own most prized possessions is a gold cigarette case bearing the inscription, 'To Bill Daniels – with Sincere Appreciation, Greta Garbo'.

She was usually friendly with the other actors and would often make jokes or play games. No one felt she was untouchable. She was often quite gay, and so were we all. How she gained her reputation as the 'Sphinx of the Screen' or 'The Woman Who Walks Alone' is a mystery to me! I remember one incident when we were shooting *The Kiss*. For the whole of the first day, Lew Ayres had been called upon to make passionate love to Garbo. When we finished at the end of that day, she turned to the director, Jacques Feyder, and said, 'I wonder if you would mind introducing me to this boy – we have not met?' By some oversight, Lew had not been introduced to the star! During the rest of the picture it was her chief delight to turn to him after every love scene and enquire with a smile, 'Have we met?'

We also had a laugh over a scene in *Romance*. During this an organ-grinder's monkey had come to Garbo's window and handed her a tin cup containing a message from her lover. But as she reached for the cup, the monkey bit her. For a moment everyone on the set was horrified. What would she do? She was neither flustered nor angry. She lifted the monkey's skirt, spanked him lightly, and

Previous Page: *A still which graphically illustrates William Daniels' use of lighting – from* Flesh and the Devil. *Daniels is standing at the rear*

said, 'Stop that!' That impromptu episode stayed in the picture.

And she also enjoyed a laugh at her own expense as she proved when we were making *Susan Lennox: Her Fall and Rise*. During the recording of one long scene everything was completely ruined by a plaintive mewing. The culprit was soon discovered – a tiny, unhappy little kitten. Garbo then demanded that it should be given to her to nurse. She played with the animal all the afternoon, laughing at its tricks, and when the day's work was finished, picked it up in her arms. 'I tink we go 'ome now,' she remarked in a perfect burlesque of that phrase so popularly attributed to her!

Garbo was a very understanding person. That's what was in those eyes. In my early years I was strongly drawn to my grandmother, who seemed to have the most beautiful feeling for people and life. It amazed me to find that same feeling in Garbo, a very young woman. The secret of her success was her complete concentration on her roles. She would arrive on the set in full character when she began a picture, and remain so until it was finished. She allowed nothing to break the spell – that is why her performances are so uniformly good.

She took direction very easily. Whatever the director demanded, she responded whole-heartedly. Should the director be in any way indecisive about his plans, she was always ready with suggestions. I have never known anyone to work as rapidly and readily as Garbo. She had a great appreciation of artistic effort, and was willing to take unusual pains in the making of a difficult scene. She was patient beyond description during the arranging of cameras and lights for an unusual effect. Before the picture began she knew her script thoroughly. She would arrive promptly at nine in the morning ready to start work on the minute. She did not like to work later than five, but if the occasion demanded that she worked through the night for night scenes, then she would absent herself from the studio the day before and the day after that work.

To this day, I think she is seen at her best in big close-ups – when her eyes tell the story. The saddest thing in my career was that I was never able to photograph her in colour. I begged the studio. I felt I had to get those incredible blue eyes in colour, but they said no. The process at the time was cumbersome and expensive, and the pictures were already making money. I still feel sad about that.

Greta Garbo HOLLYWOOD WILL SEE ME NO MORE!

The year 1932 saw Garbo consolidate her world-wide fame with three more important films. These were the exotic story of the famous World War I Germany spy, *Mata Hari* (with Ramon Novarro), a stylish adaptation of Luigi Pirandello's play, *As You Desire Me* (co-starring Erich von Stroheim), and the star-studded drama of *Grand Hotel* based on Vicki Baum's best-selling novel and play which also featured John and Lionel Barrymore, Joan Crawford and Wallace Beery. The demands of making these pictures one after another again placed an enormous strain on Garbo's health and strength (also favourite topics with Hollywood gossip columnists) and no one could wonder that she felt in need of a rest come the summer. There was also the little matter of her contract being due for renewal. This famous agreement which Harry Edington had made with MGM in 1927 had seen her complete seventeen films and become a dollar millionairess. Rumours were naturally soon abroad in Hollywood that Garbo was not going to sign another contract; that she was tired of making films in America, and as she was now financially independent she might well return to live in Sweden.

Speculation ran like wildfire through the press, fuelled by a terse announcement from Harry Edington in July that his client was shortly leaving for 'an indefinite stay in Sweden'. And sure enough Garbo sailed away to Stockholm where she saw out the rest of the year in the company of her mother and brother and a small group of intimates. As the months passed, opinions began to harden that Garbo would indeed never return to Hollywood. And in October these appeared to be confirmed when Harry Edington released a syndicated story bearing the star's name and declaring that *Grand Hotel*, which was just about to be released would be her grand finale. Hollywood, Garbo declared, would see her no more! Readers everywhere studied the article with a mixture of fascination and incredulity. Was the great Garbo *really* going to turn her back on the world she had conquered with her unique beauty and great talent . . . ?

A ravishing still of Garbo from **Mata Hari** *(1932)*

182

Garbo goes blonde for her role opposite Erich von Stroheim in As You Desire Me *(1932)*

Overleaf: Admirers were *falling at Garbo's feet on set as well as off – from* Grand Hotel *(1932)*

Now that I have left Hollywood behind me and said 'Good-bye' to all that it implies, I can think more or less calmly of the last hectic months, when the making of *Grand Hotel* occupied every moment of my waking hours.

Here in the quiet surroundings of the Swedish country-side it is possible to indulge in some afterthoughts of Hollywood, to look back without bitterness on the strange kaleidoscope of the motion-picture world and the part which I played on its brightly illuminated stage. Although there were times when I rebelled violently against conditions in Hollywood and the factory-system of film-production in force there, my memories are on the whole pleasant ones.

It would be idle to pretend, of course, that I was equally well pleased with each and every picture I made. Under such a system, an actress is bound to be miscast occasionally, and I was no exception to the rule. That does not mean, however, that I was dissatisfied with my role in *Grand Hotel*. Here, if ever, is what we call in the theatrical profession, 'an actor's picture'. Each characterisation is dramatic to its fingertips. I am proud to have been associated with it.

Yet, what misgivings were felt by some of those engaged on the task of transferring it to the screen! For the first time, the studio was trying the experiment of assembling stars with the biggest drawing-power all in one cast. They were, so to speak, recklessly 'putting all their eggs in one basket'. Pessimists predicted they would have a fine omelette for their pains!

Others said that stars like Joan Crawford, the Barrymores, Wallace Beery, and myself, who were accustomed to pocketing the entire *kudos* of a production, would resent having to share the honours, if any. We would not tolerate, they croaked, the intrusion of a rival star, intent upon 'hogging the camera' and 'stealing the picture'. A lot of nonsense was talked about the jealousy and bad feeling the new system would generate, of the tact and diplomacy required to keep the peace and weld four or five temperamental players into a harmonious whole.

It never seemed to occur to anyone that film stars might welcome the opportunity of playing together! Our opinion in the matter was never asked. Yet why, in heaven's name, should we object? No artist worth her salt willingly plays with a weak supporting cast. It is an axiom for the theatre that a strong cast adds to, rather than detracts from, the performance of the principals. For my part, therefore, I was delighted at the prospect of appearing in a picture with players of such brilliance. It put me on my mettle, and impelled me to give the best that was in me.

I should have been happier still if – in the interests of artistic fidelity – I had been allowed to adhere more strictly to Vicki Baum's delineation of Grusinskaya as a worn-out, weary little Russian dancer whose grace and gifts are fading. But I suppose such freedom of expression was too much to expect from my erstwhile lords and masters at Hollywood!

Contrary to the general belief that exhibitions of 'temperament' were frequent, I enjoyed working with my distinguished players, and I attribute the film's general excellence not to the much-advertised 'star-system' but to the magnificent 'team-spirit' of director and troupe.

The true artist revels in the contact with kindred spirits. From such contact springs the genuine daemonic fire, the creative energy, which infects everyone engaged on the production, and results in that rare something known as 'inspiration'. If the actors in this picture were jealous of anything, it was of the reputations we had built up through the years – our reputations as actors. We had to appear and re-appear like recurring *motifs* in a symphony; we had to symbolise our cross-section of life rather than mirror it. That meant the submerging – as far as was artistically possible – of our own personalities. The play had to become 'the thing', and we, the players, its puppets.

Director Edmund Goulding set the pace, and the rest of us knit ourselves into a team as compact and as interdependent as any stock company. To achieve success and truth, it had to be; and it was. Why, even dear John Barry-

THE GARB—000,000
£3,000-a-Week Contract for
Film Star

more forgot to pose – and when one has said that one has said almost all!

Perhaps our success will persuade other studios to adopt the experiment of assembling an all-star cast, to form permanent groups of star-power players within each unit, and so create a genuine team-spirit, or *esprit de corps*. Unfortunately, *esprit de corps* is literally a foreign word in Hollywood. When translated, it means too often simply 'a team of stars', a multiplication of star-power, harnessed to the service of the box-office for the purpose of 'pulling in' the patrons by means of a gigantic 'ballyhoo' campaign.

This sort of thing – already developed to the *n*th degree of proficiency in Hollywood – is the very antithesis of the team-spirit that has for so long been a feature of legitimate stage practice, something that has grown up by the long association of players. It is because I wish to recapture this precious spirit of comradeship and professional pride that I have decided to enter the theatrical production field myself. I have taken control of the Intima Teatern, Stockholm's smartest intimate theatre, and propose to open the season with Naima Wifstrand, the operatic singer, who appeared in the London revival of *The Dollar Princess*.

After all, there is still a great deal that the stage can teach its illegitimate child, the cinema, and unless the time-honoured traditions and team-spirit of the theatrical profession – which can do so much to smooth the path of the sorely beset star – are henceforth incorporated as part of the cinema code, Hollywood is doomed, and will see me no more. In that case *Grand Hotel* is my *grande finale*!

A rare Garbo press conference – and news of her spectacular film deal made in 1933

Laurence Olivier

THE QUEEN I COULD NOT CONQUER

It is an intriguing fact to ponder: but if Garbo had not read a biography about an eccentric seventeenth century Swedish monarch, Queen Christina, while she was on holiday in Sweden, would she have remained true to her word and parted company with Hollywood almost a decade before she actually did so? As soon as she had finished the book, she became captivated with the idea of making a film about the Queen's life. The biography had actually been given to her by a close friend in Hollywood named Salka Viertel, a former actress turned screenwriter, and naturally Garbo turned straight away to her with this idea. Mrs Viertel began work on a script immediately and as soon as Garbo saw the finished product announced that if MGM would film it she would sign a new contract with them. Her terms were demanding, to be sure: she would make just two pictures a year for the studio at an annual fee of £156,000 — a figure that would make her the highest paid actress in the business. MGM eventually agreed.

In April 1933 Garbo re-crossed the Atlantic so that work on *Queen Christina* could begin. News of her return excited enormous interest: all talk of retirement ceased. The Queen of Hollywood was about to start a new reign playing a queen! The excitement was heightened still more when it was announced that John Gilbert was once again to star with Garbo. The couple who had created a thousand headlines five years before were about to be reunited! Now, though, their circumstances were somewhat different. Garbo was the international star at the height of her popularity, while Gilbert — whose thin, high-pitched voice had sounded rather ludicrous when the talkies arrived — was fading fast. A rumour flew around Hollywood that Garbo had asked for Gilbert in order to repay his earlier kindness and save his flagging career. The actual story, however, was rather less romantic though equally dramatic. There had, in fact, been other candidates before John Gilbert for the role of Don Antonio, the Spanish ambassador with whom Queen Christina falls in love — including a very promising young English actor named Laurence Olivier who had actually been signed for the part and brought to Hollywood to begin work.

But in the following article, written in 1935, Olivier — later Sir Laurence and then Lord Olivier — tells the noted film critic Virginia Maxwell of *Photoplay Magazine* just how his chance to star opposite Garbo was frustrated and John Gilbert obtained what was to prove a momentary revival in his film fortunes before his dissolute life-style brought on a heart-attack and his sudden death in 1936.

Laurence Olivier — a misspelled publicity photograph of 1933

189

190

KINGSTON COLLEGE OF TECHNOLOGY
CANNAUGHON RDAD, SOUTH KINGSTON-ON-SEA

Once in a lifetime, out of the kaleidoscope which is Hollywood, there comes an epic real-life drama, a quirk of fate so strange that it is almost unbelievable. This is what really happened to John Gilbert. A chance remark, tossed lightly by an assistant electrician and intended to be funny, was the turning point in John Gilbert's life, the axle which fate supplied to lift him high on the wheel of good fortune once again – to play opposite Garbo – from the depths of movie oblivion to which he had sunk in the last years.

For the first time, this inside story is now told. By the actor who was brought six thousand miles on contract to play opposite Garbo in *Queen Christina*, only to lose the role to Gilbert. Why? How did it happen? It's a fascinating story, one of the few real-life dramas of the studio which come from Hollywood only too infrequently. To understand the great moment which fate threw to John Gilbert, we'll have to go back a few months.

Garbo's new contract, in which she is permitted complete okay of who shall play as her lover and who shall not, had just been signed on her return from Europe. Garbo looked at many 'tests' and could not find the type of lover she demanded in *Queen Christina*. Then they brought in films and ran them off for the great Garbo to study. *Westward Passage*, in which Ann Harding was starred, flashed upon the screen of MGM's private projection room. In it appeared a personable young English actor – Laurence Olivier. Garbo signalled for the film to stop. And in one queenly command, Laurence Olivier was decided as the man to play her screen lover in *Queen Christina*.

Metro consulted their files. He wasn't in Hollywood. Olivier had returned to London and was starring in a Brit-

A rare photograph of Garbo and John Gilbert re-united before filming began on Queen Christina

SOUTHEND COLLEGE OF TECHNOLOGY
CARNARVON ROAD, SOUTHEND-ON-SEA

ish stage play. He had always been a stage star and pictures had been merely a fling for him. London Metro offices contacted Olivier that very night. And before the first light of dawn had pierced London's famous fog, Laurence Olivier was signing his name on the dotted line to one of the most enviable picture contracts ever offered. It meant giving up his role on the stage. It meant a six thousand mile jaunt, across sea and land, to Hollywood. He made the trip willingly – eagerly, followed by the trumpet and fanfare of a world-wide publicity campaign. Olivier was Garbo's new screen lover, and the world must know.

What happened from then on is Olivier's own story – told exclusively for the first time to *Photoplay*.

'The day I was introduced to Greta,' he said, in his charming way, 'I realised at once she was going to be difficult to know. She's shy as an antelope. And when I tried to warm her to my own personality with a little conversation, she answered only in monosyllables. Garbo is really the mythical person people have imagined,' he explained quickly. 'She seems to live entirely within herself, unaffected by any of the little things to which most mortals are humanised. A rare, exotic person, yet so different from any other woman in the world, that she is a fascinating mixture of shyness and mystery.

'Garbo was wearing loose lounging pyjamas, a cigarette hung between her slender fingers, a script of the picture carried constantly under one arm. She never rehearses. But for this unusual role, the studio executives had persuaded her to do some rehearsing before the actual "takes". The stage was set for our most important scene – when, as Don Antonio, I meet Garbo in her boudoir at the inn and there discover the warm, tender woman beneath the boyish masquerade. And this is the part of my story I shall always look back upon with a mixture of amazement and disappointment.

'The director explained that I was to come forward, grasp Garbo's slender body tenderly, look into her eyes and, in the gesture, awaken the passion within her – that passion for which she is later willing to give up the Swedish throne. I went into my role giving it everything I had. But at the touch of my hand Garbo became frigid. I could feel the sudden tautness of her; her eyes as stony and expressionless as if she were a woman of marble. Rouben Mamoulian, the director who knew exactly what he wanted, came quietly over and spoke to Garbo. He asked her to warm up to me – to try to bring some fire into her eyes – some expression of tenderness into the lovely curves of her rich, warm mouth.

'We tried it again. But Garbo was unmoved. She, the great actress, whom everyone expected to go into this tender scene with convincing abandon, was as frigid to my embrace as if she were a woman of stone. Mamoulian came over again. He asked me to talk to Garbo – off the set. To try to break down this intangible barrier which had risen between us; these cross currents of magnetism completely out of harmony with each other. We walked a little; smoked together, tried to talk small talk. Then we came back and went into the scene again. Garbo froze up as before. The director, realising with his keen sense of screen values that Garbo's attitude would register cold, was desperate. Suddenly he flung down the script, called a halt on everything and turned to his assistants. "In heaven's name, is there any man Garbo *will* warm to?" he cried.

'One of the electricians, trying to be funny, shouted that John Gilbert was the only man Garbo ever went ga-ga over. "Get him! Get him here," the director shouted. "Get Gilbert and let's get some emotion into this scene!"

'They sent for Gilbert then. To use his presence merely as a stimulant to Garbo's emotional depth. I took off my costume and John Gilbert got into it. As Don Antonio, he looked the part. And as I stepped aside, ready for Gilbert to warm Garbo to the role, an amazing thing happened, Garbo's face softened; into her eyes came a strange, beautiful light. Something seemed to be happening deep down inside her. A magic spell, this emotion which John Gilbert stirred within her when he took Garbo in his arms and whispered those tender phrases.

'We were watching the real thing, an astonishing reaction – Garbo's thrilling to the man she once had loved. The director was delighted. And what was to have been merely a rehearsal between Gilbert and Garbo became a real shot. I knew at that moment that I had lost the part I had come six thousand miles to play. But I willingly relinquished it to Gilbert for he was clearly the man who could conquer this Queen.'

THE MOST BEAUTIFUL FACE I EVER SAW

The combination of Garbo and John Gilbert provided the director of *Queen Christina*, Rouben Mamoulian, with just the chemistry he needed to coax memorable performances from both of them. But this time it was not the Garbo-Gilbert partnership that intrigued the gossip columnists while filming was taking place – but that of Garbo and Mamoulian. For no sooner had the two of them been seen dining together and out dancing on the famous Sunset Strip in the evenings, than a romance was being predicted. Newspapers and magazines declared in banner headlines across their front pages, 'Garbo Falls in Love!' while *Modern Screen*'s writer Mary Ann Stevens spoke for them all when she confided: 'The drama of that almost legendary figure out of history, the royal Queen Christina who masqueraded as a boy, now being enacted before the cameras of Culver City, cannot be half so exciting as the thing that has happened behind the cameras during the filming of the picture. Garbo has fallen in love. This time, with her new director, Rouben Mamoulian. Only a few people on the MGM lot know of it,' Miss Stevens added breathlessly, 'the privileged few who work daily on the set with Garbo.'

In actual fact, no one on the set knew anything of the kind. The director and star had certainly formed a friendship based on mutual respect – Garbo undoubtedly admired the determined, cultured and imaginative Russian-born Mamoulian – but their out-of-studio meetings were for no other purpose than for two professionals to reach a better understanding of one another. Garbo, predictably, never denied these allegations; but Mamoulian did, most emphatically. For him filming *Queen Christina* was a fascinating and rewarding experience which brought him critical acclaim and confirmed his reputation as a leading Hollywood director. Just what his real feelings towards Garbo were at this time he has set straight in the following interview he gave *American Film* magazine in January 1983.

Rouben Mamoulian

195

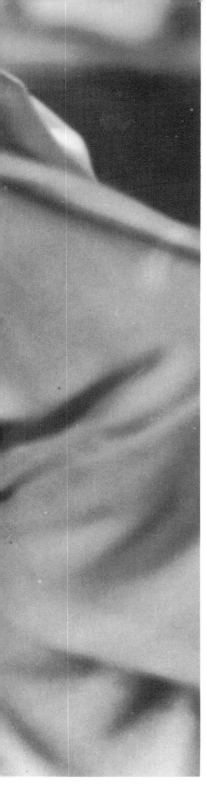

I had never met Garbo before the filming of *Queen Christina*. I was working at Paramount and had just finished a picture with Marlene Dietrich called *Song of Songs*. Then MGM – Louis B. Mayer – called me and said, 'We'd like you to direct the next film of Greta Garbo. We have an idea about Queen Christina of Sweden.' They sent me the script and I liked the idea. I told them, 'We will have to do some rewriting.' They said, 'OK.'

MGM was a producer's studio. The director would finish the film, and then the producer and executives would come in and do whatever they felt was necessary. I said to Mr Mayer, 'I can't work that way. At Paramount I was producer-director; I never had any interference. I had the final say.' Walter Wanger, the producer, was from Paramount and a good friend of mine. So I said, 'I would like Mr Wanger's name to be in my contract.' And Mayer said, 'We can't do that. Suppose he dies?' I said, 'Well, if he dies, then I become the producer. I will not take it with another producer.' He finally agreed to this.

Then I asked, 'First I would like to meet Miss Garbo – why don't you ask her if she would like to see a first cut of *Song of Songs*, which I just finished with Dietrich?' She said she would like to come and see it. She liked the picture. She would appreciate it so much if I would direct *Queen Christina*. And I said, 'Well, I would like to, very much, but there is something that I have to take up with you. I understand that when you are doing an intimate scene with an actor, everybody has to leave the stage, including the director.' She said, 'Yes. Clarence Brown used to go and have a sandwich.' I replied, 'I can't work that way. I am there every second.' She thought about it, and said, 'Well, all right, I will agree to that.'

So we worked on the script. I got S. N. Behrman, a very fine playwright from New York, to work on the dialogue. Garbo never had such an extensive dialogue in any of her former films. We came on the set, and I took a scene in the Queen's study with Ian Keith, Lewis Stone and Garbo. I said, 'Now we will rehearse.' Garbo said to me, 'Oh, I don't rehearse. If I rehearse, I become stale. If you take more than one take, I become empty inside.' So I said, 'Well, Miss Garbo, this is incredible. Let's make a deal. I'll do it your way. If that works out it will be marvellous, because I will earn the reputation of the fastest-shooting director in Hollywood. I'll get through the picture in four weeks instead of eight. But if it doesn't work out you will try to do it my way.' She said, 'It will work out.'

So I rehearsed the two men for an hour and a half. Then she came in and I told her, 'You start here, you do this, you go there, you do this.' 'Fine.' And so we made a first take. Afterward I said, 'Well, how do you feel about it?' And she said, 'Fine! Fine!' As she was about to walk past me, she stopped and said, 'Well, how do *you* feel about it?' I said, 'No good. It's all wrong.' I added, 'We made a deal, we'll rehearse.' She said, 'Believe me, I'll get worse.' So I rehearsed the three of them for over an hour, and with each rehearsal she said, 'I'm getting worse.'

After an hour's rehearsal, she said, 'I am completely empty, there is nothing there at all.' I said, 'That's all right. We will make take two.' This take was followed by take three, take four, take five, up to eight takes. I said, 'Print take eight. And print take one. Now, Miss Garbo, tomorrow morning take one – yours – and take eight – the one I like – will be in the projection room. You go in there alone. You see these two takes and then you tell me which one I should use in the picture, and I promise to abide by your judgment.' She started walking out. Then she came back, leaned close to my ear, and whispered, 'Please do not print take one.' From then on it was wonderful.

One of the problems on the picture was in the scene when she arrives on horseback and sees the Spanish ambassador's carriage stuck in the snow. There was John Gilbert with heavy furs on, Akim Tamiroff, and two others. I said, 'Now you ride in and you see them struggling; they don't know how to get the wheels from under the snow, because they are from sunny Spain. It's funny; you laugh.' And she said, 'I can't laugh.' I said, 'I hear you laughing in life like a little girl.' She said, 'Yes, but not on the screen. I can cry, I can smile, I can go hysterical, I can

198

get angry, but I cannot laugh.' I thought about that and I said, 'Go rest and don't worry about it.' She went off and I told the four actors, 'Look, you are working on the carriage and she rides in. Now turn around and make funny faces to me, you know, the way kids do.' Now when Garbo came and got on her horse, I told her, 'I want you to promise me one thing. You ride in, and no matter what happens, you carry on with the dialogue.' She said, 'Well, have I ever failed to do that?' I said, 'No, but I just want to be sure that you carry it through.' She said, 'Of course I will.' I said, 'OK.' My camera was set on Garbo's close-up. So she rode in and they turned around and off she went: the most beautiful laughter! This was the first time Garbo laughed on the screen.

There are actors who are intuitive and actors who reason. Sometimes they are a combination of both, but that's rare. The greatest thing is intuition. For instance, with Garbo, I would say to her, 'This mood is like the purple sunset, when the leaves turn their shadows, and now and then a yellow leaf falls down.' She would say, 'Oh, I know.' And people would ask. 'What is going on?'

Mamoulian has also spoken about the final scene in *Queen Christina* which many critics and fans alike believe to be Garbo's finest moment on the screen. As well as being her most famous. As she is sailing into exile from Sweden, the Queen stands in the bow of the ship staring enigmatically into the distance. Mamoulian explained how he obtained these moments of sheer cinema magic to *American Classic Screen* in January 1977:

Prior to shooting the last close-up of the final scene in the film, I said to Garbo, 'I want your face to be a blank sheet of paper. I want the writing to be done by every member of the audience.' My reasons for making that statement are these. It bears directly on the basic principle that in the art of the theatre, whether on stage or on film, we have before us an audience. That means that not only do you have people sitting there looking at something, but you seek to involve them in what is happening. You want to stir the deepest emotions and the deepest reactions. Your goal is active participation, not just the static act of people sitting and watching a stage or screen. That to me is a very important element to strive toward, and that is what I always do, both on the stage and screen.

Here you have the story of Queen Christina, who abdicates her throne because she loves the Spanish Ambassador, and when she comes to join him on the sailing boat

Overleaf: One of the most famous moments from a Garbo film – the finale to Queen Christina

he dies from fatal wounds inflicted in a duel. I thought about this scene involving her reaction in terms of dialogue. You couldn't express it so there's a minimum of verbiage in that last sequence. It is all imagery. At the end I had Garbo walk to the bow of the boat. The question was what Garbo should do. There are times when no matter what you do, part of the audience will think it is wrong, and I did not want that, especially at the end of the film. I wanted the audience engrossed. For instance, if I had told her to cry, some of the audience would say that she was a weak woman. If I had had her smile, many would ask, 'What is wrong with her? She just lost her lover.' No matter what one would choose to do, a number of the members of the audience would think it wrong.

I decided that the only recipe for holding all of the audience was to have Garbo do nothing. Through visual imagery the audience would be seasoned so that when it came to the final close-up of her face, they could write in the emotions. If a person felt she was heartbroken, then that was what the person would see. If someone felt that she was serene, then that is what that person would see, for there would be no contradiction in Garbo's face. The spectator was able to write his own ending, his own feelings. Those are the really high moments of the theatre collage where you can get an audience so involved that it can become creative.

I am often asked why I think Garbo has continued to have such a charismatic hold not only on her own generation but subsequent ones as well. To begin with the most obvious pragmatic qualifications, she has the most beautiful face that ever was. No matter how you light her or what angle you take she photographs beautifully. It's an incredible face. Also, she is a totally intuitive actress. She is not subject to logic or reasoning, so that when you direct her, there's no point in talking logically about what that scene is. You talk to her about the fine nuances and subtle emotions of a scene, and with her she understands with her intuition what is in my intuition. When you put these two elements together you have a charismatic result. It is personality plus what she does.

The ultimate qualification for a star that is glamorous or any person that is charismatic is that the audience sees more than there is. Now how does that happen? It happens because of this magical quality of stirring people's imaginations.

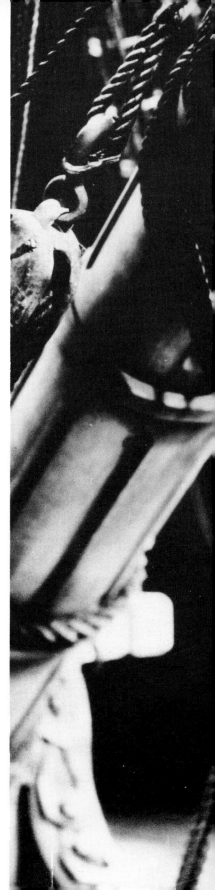

Cecilia Parker

WHAT GARBO TAUGHT ME

The scriptwriter Salka Viertel who had been instrumental in getting Garbo back before the film cameras for *Queen Christina*, also suggested and co-wrote her next picture, *The Painted Veil* (1934), which was based on a novel by Somerset Maugham set in China and describing the affair of a doctor's wife (Garbo) and a diplomatic attaché (George Brent). Herbert Marshall played the third member of the eternal triangle whose marriage is finally saved when a cholera epidemic reunites him with his fickle wife. Once again there were stories of an off-screen romance between Garbo and George Brent which proved without foundation. There can be little dispute that *The Painted Veil* is one of Garbo's least distinguished films and it did not fare well at the box office. However, acting in the picture was a young actress whose life and career were to be irrevocably changed by contact with Garbo. She was Cecilia Parker who was plucked from the ranks of MGM starlets where she had been playing the heroine in a series of Westerns, to appear as Garbo's sister in *The Painted Veil*. The experience of acting with the great star made an enormous impression on Cecilia, and in the following article which she wrote for *Film Pictorial* in January 1935 she gives a unique picture of Garbo from the viewpoint of a supporting player.

Cecilia Parker on the set of **The Painted Veil** *with her 'teacher', Garbo (1934)*

Garbo made me what I am today. She is responsible for my being on the screen.

I'd thought of becoming a film actress when I was at school. I suppose almost all girls brought up in Hollywood think about it. Then I saw Garbo on the screen. I saw her again and again and again. I knew that I would have to follow in her footsteps, however humbly I might walk.

And so I started in. I was just sixteen when I signed with Central Casting. I secured extra work. One day a casting director noticed me and offered me a screen test. I guess it was successful because I became a 'heroine' in several Western pictures. Then MGM signed me to a long-term contract. Shortly thereafter they needed a blonde girl who resembled Greta Garbo enough to play her sister in *Painted Veil*.

Just imagine – you girls in your teens – how you would feel if you were told, suddenly, that you were to work with Garbo. Why, if anyone had intimated that, when I was in school a few years ago, I should have thought he had gone completely insane.

Garbo didn't talk to me very much. She doesn't talk to anyone very much. She doesn't need to. Which is one of the many things I learned from her – how much time and energy most of us waste in silly chatter that means nothing. There is something more potent in Garbo's silence than in the words most of us pour forth in a week. Hers are what my mother calls 'telling silences'.

Garbo and I did have one conversation. It was about mountains. I happened to be saying that I have a little cabin up in the hills where I like to go off by myself. Garbo overheard me and said that she loves mountains, too. She told me what they mean to her – grandeur and everlasting

That famous face – a still from The Painted Veil *(1934)*

Overleaf: *George Brent, who was also rumoured to have fallen in love with Garbo, on the set of* The Painted Veil

patience and a dwarfing of the silly frets and fevers of little human beings. I think that she was, unconsciously, describing herself in a symbolic way. There is something cool and remote and unassailable about her that does dwarf the frets and fevers of most of us.

I'd just been a little girl full of crazy notions when I started to work with her. I'd had most of the usual fantastic ideas. I thought I should act sort of temperamental, thinking it made an impression. I took on, unconsciously and sometimes a little consciously, the mannerisms and characteristics of stars on the screen. I thought it was all right to be late on the set now and then. I'd seen some stars keep a company waiting for an hour or more and thought it indicated a certain superiority, a defiance of rules and regulations which are just for 'ordinary people', not actresses.

Garbo taught me to be myself, to behave according to the dictates of my own nature. She taught me that to be true to yourself is to be not only a great artiste but also a great human being.

It wasn't really like me to put on airs, to be excitable and fluttery, to be late when I'd been brought up to respect punctuality. I hate crowds. I never go to big parties. I really could say 'I tink I go home' myself – and mean it. In fact, I often do. But most girls experiment with themselves for a time, try different airs and graces and poses, as they try on clothes. It's all right if the airs and graces don't stick and become a part of you.

She taught me not to borrow from other people. She taught me not to borrow their mannerisms, their eccentricities, their fads, any more than I would borrow their clothes, their cars, their jewels and keep them for myself.

Garbo is always on time on the set – to the minute. She would make anyone else seem pretty silly if he were not at least equally prompt. She taught me consideration for others. Like many girls, I thought that actresses were sort of special, were exempt from conventional creeds and customs. Garbo taught me how young and ignorant that point of view really is. By her unfailing promptitude, by her courtesy to the men working on the sets, by being always letter-perfect in her lines and by her generosity to those working with her, she gave me a standard I know I shall never lose.

She has no petty fears about footage and camera angles and whether or not she is getting more, as star, than members of the supporting cast. She does her work thoroughly and she expects others to do the same and may the best

206

man win! She taught me poise, too. She taught me how much more beautiful and impressive it is to bear yourself quietly, with dignity and without circus show-off tactics. And she taught me how to relax. Between scenes Garbo always retired to her dressing-room or sat on the sidelines, watching, relaxed in every nerve and muscle. She can be more still than any human being I have ever seen. *Her composure is more beautiful than the most animated motion. When she goes into an emotional scene, she is like a being charged and recharged; she is all alive and there is fire and force and depth behind it. She hasn't frittered it all away on nothings.* She taught me to save myself for emotional scenes, in real life as well as on the screen. She taught me not to break myself up into little pieces for trivialities.

She taught me to be immaculate, which is quite a different thing from being 'dressy'. I have never seen anyone more immaculate than Garbo. Her shining, brushed hair, her clean strong hands, without nail polish or benefit of beauty parlour – if ever I thought it amusing to paint my nails like an Indian's, or frizz my hair or wear extreme styles, I got well over it, thanks to her.

She taught me the beauty and the wisdom of tact. She never gives advice to younger, newer players who are working on her pictures. I know some actresses and actors who are always telling you that you should do a scene this way or that way or hadn't you, perhaps, better try it the other way; they really serve mostly to make you self-conscious. Garbo is silent. She never gives one an inferiority complex. She seems to expect people to live up to what they are supposed to do.

I can't ever be like Garbo physically even though I did resemble her enough to play her sister. I do have almost exactly the same colouring, though. People tell me we have something of the same quality in our voices; I am short, whereas she is tall. I have a round face, though I have hopes that it will thin out in time. Even though I can't look much like her, I can try to be like her inside and I do. I know that I sound like a Garbo fan. Well, I *am* a Garbo fan. Of course, being a Garbo fan means loving and admiring Garbo and only by intense admiration are we ever stirred enough to try to be like the object of our admiration.

I know that I've lost all temptation to copy or imitate anyone. Please don't misunderstand – I don't mean that I'm trying to look or to act like Garbo. That would be ridiculous. If I were trying that, then Garbo wouldn't really have taught me anything at all. No, what I am trying to do is to be as honest in my work and in my personal life as Garbo is in hers, to have in my way the same integrity and courage she has in hers.

She taught me not to be afraid of anything – not even humdrum practical truths about oneself. I'm a good cook, for instance. When I'm not working I keep house for my mother, my brother and myself. And when I say that I keep house, I mean keep house, not just direct a servant. We don't have one. We did have one for a time but she made mother so nervous that we let her go. I cook and do some washing and ironing and just have a woman in to do the heavy laundry.

A few weeks ago a director called me from the studio and asked me to come over for an interview. He said, 'Are you busy? What are you doing?' I told him I was working in the house. He thought he hadn't heard me right and he said, 'I don't get you – you're doing *what*?' I told him again and he laughed and said that he didn't believe me. But I was. He should have seen me and he'd have believed me all right – I had on an old house dress and no shoes and stockings and my hair and hands and face were a sight!

Well, there was a time when I wouldn't have admitted to this. I should have thought that a film actress shouldn't let it out that she even knows there are houses cleaned and meals to be cooked. But if Garbo talked she would admit practical truths about herself, I'm sure of that. She probably doesn't scrub floors nowadays, perhaps she never did. But what I'm trying to explain is that Garbo would never be ashamed of any honest work she did, no matter what.

I hope things work out happily and successfully. If they don't, I hope I have learned from Garbo to take loneliness with courage, and heartbreak with dignity.

SOME SECRETS OF 'MOSCOW'

Tallulah Bankhead

As I hope has been made evident already, it was not only supporting players, co-stars, cameramen, scriptwriters and directors who came to admire Garbo's talent, but also other famous Hollywood stars like herself. Malice towards one another has often been a notable attribute among film stars over the years, but Garbo seems almost unique in that virtually everyone was in awe of her beauty and ability, and quite willing to accept her foibles in demanding seclusion and privacy rather than parading herself in the usual manner for the benefit of press and public. Typical among these stars was Tallulah Bankhead, the beautiful if more outgoing and occasionally outrageous actress who already had a multitude of fans around the world. Yet like millions of others she was desperately keen to meet the legendary Garbo. Her opportunity came through her friendship with Salka and Berthold Viertel, and when the two stars did meet, Tallulah confessed later than she was so nervous she 'clowned outrageously'. Nevertheless, the two became friends, meeting together and dining quite frequently.

In her autobiography written later she declared with typical aplomb, 'Forget all the bilge about Garbo. She's excessively shy. When at ease with people who do not look upon her as something begat by the Sphinx and Frigga, the Norse Goddess of the sky, she can be as much fun as the next girl.' Many years prior to this, in April 1934, Tallulah had written in *Film World* magazine how she came to meet Garbo the first time, and how their friendship developed, giving a particularly interesting portrait of Garbo from the viewpoint of another Hollywood super-star. (An interesting fact mentioned by Tallulah Bankhead is Garbo's use of pseudonyms when travelling. During her life time she used a whole variety of these: one day she would be Gussie Berger, on another Mary Holmquist, Jane Emerson, Alice Smith and even on a few occasions, Karl Lund. Her most frequently used, though, was the simple and unassuming Harriet Brown.)

Tallulah Bankhead, another of Garbo's famous film-star friends

211

Hollywood may give a superior smile when 'fan' mail or gallery girls are mentioned, but there is one person who can turn the tables on Hollywood. Garbo commands hero-worship even from the 'stars' who are themselves receiving thousands of letters per day from admirers.

This week I am going to tell you about my friendship with that wonderful Queen of the Screen – the incomparable Garbo. It is time that the truth was told about a ridiculous story that was circulated after my arrival in Hollywood. It was said that she turned her back on me when we met. Nothing could be further from the truth. Just as Gary Cooper was my favourite film actor, so Garbo was the one woman artist whom I was determined to meet if it were possible. And this is how it all came about.

I was making a film in New York – a thoroughly bad film – and Berthold Viertel, the great German producer, came there to do what he could to improve the parts that had already been 'shot' and arrange for re-takes. His wife, Salka, came with him. She is an actress with a big reputation in Germany, and a great friend of Greta Garbo. It was she who wrote *Queen Christina* for her, and she has written other successes.

When the re-takes had been finished, Viertel and Salka decided to have a holiday in New York, and it was then that we got to know each other really well. They are charming people with an attractive trace of accent. Her English is a sort of poetry, full of picturesque phraseology, and Bertold, for some reason best known to himself, always called me 'The Sun'.

Anyway, they gave me a divine time in New York. At that time I had no idea that I was going to Hollywood, and the fact that arrangements had been made came as a very

Curious – but unmistakably Garbo once again!

213

pleasant surprise. We all decided to travel together, and it was on the train that tongues started wagging about Garbo and myself. Salka had mentioned to someone that both of us were great friends of hers.

'Poor Salka,' said someone maliciously, 'Tallulah coming in the front door and Greta running out the back door without even time to slip on her mackintosh! What a life!' To which I replied, equally in jest, but it was taken seriously: 'Ha! You wait till I get to Hollywood. Garbo will ask to meet me!'

Naturally Salka was continually being pestered by people who wanted to meet Garbo. I determined, with Audrey and Kenneth Carten, who were with me, that she would never be able to accuse *us* of using her friendship in that way. The thing became almost a complex with us, and we decided that anyone who mentioned Garbo's name would have to pay the others a hundred dollars.

We soon found out that to omit Garbo's name from a Hollywood dinner-conversation is one of the most difficult things in the world. She creates so much interest that her name is continually cropping up. In the end, the fine had to be reduced from a hundred dollars to one dollar, and, even at that, it proved expensive until we hit on a plan.

You remember in *The Three Sisters* that there are three sisters whose main object in life is to visit Moscow. We decided to call Garbo by that name. 'We'll *never* see Moscow!' we used to wail. Salka thought we were all raving mad and merely said in her practical way. 'If you really want to go to Moscow, it can surely be arranged to make you happy!'

As a matter of fact, all this nonsense was quite unnecessary, for Garbo was not even in Hollywood at the time. It was to be some little time before we actually saw 'Moscow'. As it happened, Garbo's train taking her to New York on an incognito holiday crossed ours somewhere in the Middle East. She remained incognito until Walter Winchell gave away on the radio that she was staying at the St Moritz Hotel under the name of Fräulein 'Gussie' Berger.

One day Salka told us that Garbo had left New York and would arrive on the following Saturday in Hollywood. It so happened that Salka had asked us to dinner that night with the intention of taking us on to a coloured revue. Naturally, we fully expected to be put off – no 'Moscow' for us, we thought. However, the expected cancellation did not arrive and at six o'clock we went round to her house.

Greta Garbo

GRETA GARBO

CINEMA STARS

No. 42   GRETA GARBO

LLOYDS CIGARETTES

THE PAINTED VEIL

Garbo was a favourite subject in cigarette card series – as these examples show

We had a sort of tense feeling somehow, and I remarked laughingly: 'From the atmosphere of strain in this car, one might almost think we were going to see "Moscow" at last.'

On arrival I forgot all about it, and burst into the hall thinking I was alone, only to find a strange figure in lovely black pyjamas reclining on the sofa. 'Hello!' said the figure in that deep voice. Thus did we see 'Moscow' at last.

Greta was sweet to us. She helped to serve the food and was perfectly natural. I did my usual buffoonery at dinner, partly through nervousness, and was greatly relieved when Garbo said: 'This is the first dinner party I have been to in years, and I have never laughed so much in all my life!'

She is genuinely shy, and all this mystery business started quite genuinely. Naturally, it has developed into the greatest publicity stunt of all time. She would never have been allowed by Salka to meet four strange people unless she had been consulted. Her dread of strangers amounts to a disease.

Her house in Hollywood is surrounded by a tall yew hedge. The outside gate is kept locked, and even the postman has no access to the garden. Dogs prowl about in the grounds, and her swimming pool is guarded.

People have been so busy delving into her private affairs, and even bribing her servants, that these precautions have become necessary. But I will give you an example of her genuine shyness. When she was in New York she went to see Katherine Cornell in *The Barretts of Wimpole Street*. She sat through the whole play with her programme shielding her face. Thus she defeated her own object by attracting the attention of the entire audience.

Somebody told the management that she was in front. At first they refused to believe it, but eventually being satisfied, the manager asked her if she would go back and see Miss Cornell after the show. Greta was immediately seized with panic and left the theatre! On arrival home she decided that her action might be misunderstood, and went back to the theatre. And the saddest part of the story is that, when she got back, Miss Cornell refused to believe that Garbo had come to visit her! Although she received her in her dressing-room she was convinced that it was someone playing a joke on her, with the result that she was hardly cordial to her.

On another occasion she went to see the Lunts in *Reunion in Vienna*. Knowing that she had been round to see

Katherine Cornell, I asked her if she went round to see the Lunts, and she said she hadn't. 'I would have gone back,' she said, 'but I had no idea they would be glad to see me.'

Let me tell you a little about Garbo herself. She is ten times more beautiful off the screen than she is on. She has eyelashes that are too long to be true. I used to sit and wonder how she could see through them, drooping, as they do, right down over her cheek.

However, I know they are real, for I pulled them (with permission). Believe me, when you meet Garbo, everybody else seems to look like an ugly duckling. She uses no powder or make-up or rouge off the screen. But she makes up her eyelashes in the same way as she does on the sets.

And then there is the stupid story about the size of Garbo's feet. Really they are perfectly proportioned. She is a tall girl with a lovely figure, and if she had tiny feet she would look ridiculous. Imagine putting Garbo's feet on to Janet Gaynor. Well, the result would be no sillier than putting Gaynor's feet on Garbo.

Her legs are good. She has not the legs that you would expect to find on a Ziegfeld folly, but she wears flat-heeled shoes, and her legs are quite suitable to that type of footwear.

It is difficult to judge her height. It was once when I saw her with the wife of Oliver Garrett, who adapted the book of *Farewell to Arms* into a film, that she looked quite small because Mrs Oliver Garrett is six feet.

I ought to have told you that the Garretts lived next door to Salka. Their children play with one another and they are just a great family party. They have a lovely place down by the sea at Santa Monica and they invited me to a party. They were very old friends of Garbo's, but knew how shy Greta was and had not asked her.

There were at least thirty people at the party on a Saturday night. People strolled in at all hours from nine o'clock onwards. They came in just when they finished their work as is usual at Hollywood parties, which accounts for the custom of having a running buffet instead of a set meal.

During the course of the evening in the shaded lights I saw a figure like an archangel cross the hall. There was Garbo dressed all in white. I exclaimed, 'There's Garbo,' My hostess turned round completely astonished and said: 'Really? Well, she wasn't invited!' That must have been the only time on record that Garbo has gatecrashed a party. Naturally, everyone was delighted to see her and, as always happens, they stopped talking to look at her.

GRETA GARBO SPENDS MOST OF HER SPARE TIME BETWEEN PICTURES READING IN BED

216

She sensed that there was something in the atmosphere at once, and came across to where I was sitting: 'I am not spoiling the party, am I?' she said earnestly. Then she went on: 'I am so boring. People seem to stop talking when I come in.' She honestly believes that she doesn't contribute to a party.

It was a little awkward, because there was no disguising the fact that although people tried to pretend that Garbo was not monopolising the attention of everybody, she was in fact the one presence in the room that was conspicuous, although she tried not to be so. However, the shyness soon wore off and the party was a great success. Greta thoroughly enjoyed herself.

There was present at the party a woman reporter. I specially asked her not to say that I had met Garbo there. I did not want anything of that sort in the papers, because they invented such fantastic stories. They were always creating bad feeling among stars by suggesting rivalries that never existed.

Now let me tell you the only possible explanation how the story got around that Garbo turned her back on me. There was not an atom of truth in it. What really happened was this. Salka asked me to go and see her one afternoon. When I arrived I rang the bell and heard a scramble going on inside. Then when I was admitted Salka told me that Greta had been there, but had run out the back way thinking it was a stranger calling.

A few minutes later Greta phoned and when she heard that it was I who had called she spoke to me and told me how sorry she was that she had run away. 'I would not have run if I had known it was you,' she said. At that time Salka had as a guest a foreign film director. It may be that, without knowing the sequel to the story of Greta's hurried exit, he started the rumour that Greta had run away rather than meet me.

I did not see Greta for some time after that as she started making a new film. When she is filming she sees nobody outside the studio, and works so hard that she goes straight to bed, completely exhausted, at the end of the day. Towards the end of my stay in Hollywood I decided to give a party of my own, and I asked Salka to bring Garbo with her.

Well, the night of the party arrived, and the time for dinner had passed. I had quite given her up. I said to my friends Audrey and Kenneth: 'Well, I don't care if she doesn't come.' But deep down in my heart I really wanted her to come for everybody to see her. I knew that Edie would be terribly disappointed if she did not see Garbo.

Edie was behind the bar shaking cocktails. Suddenly we heard a voice away down the hall. There is only one voice like that in the world. There was no mistaking who it was. 'I am very dirty,' she said. 'I have been riding. May I come in like this?' She came in dressed in exquisitely cut jodhpurs. She looked as though she had stepped straight from the pedestal of a Greek statue. Whether she had really been within miles of a horse is a matter of speculation.

There was no shyness with her at my party. We were all very gay. We had great fun. There were only a few of us, and my coloured cook gave us a beautiful dinner. Now it is the custom in Hollywood when one has enjoyed a good dinner to go to the kitchen and congratulate the cook. My cook had been with several of the big stars over a period of years, so that film stars meant no more to her than actresses do to stage hands in the theatres. But even my cook, who was positively blasé about movie stars, got excited when she knew that Garbo was among the guests.

After dinner we all went upstairs to have coffee, when suddenly to my horror I saw my cook prancing through the drawing-room like an elated empress. I went across to Garbo and said: 'My cook is longing to meet you.' Greta congratulated her on the dinner and cook, thinking to please me, replied: 'I am glad to meet you, miss. Next to Miss Bankhead you are the finest actress on the screen.' I nearly fainted with horror, but Greta saved my embarrassment. As an example of her genuine friendliness when her shyness had been broken down, I must tell you how nice she was to my coloured butler. She smokes only one kind of cigarette. She ran out of supplies during the party. My butler offered to go for some for her. When he returned she thanked him personally and said: 'It was so nice of you to go out for me.'

I particularly wanted Ethel Barrymore to meet Garbo, but on the night of my party she had another engagement. However, when Garbo turned up I telephoned Ethel and asked her to come round. She knew instinctively that Garbo was there and came round at once. Garbo and she got on like wild-fire. Actually, I do not suppose that there is another living soul that Ethel Barrymore would cross the road to meet.

My house was always open to my friends, but on this occasion I had given strict instructions that no one was to be allowed up until I had asked Garbo if she would like to meet them. I am afraid some of them spent a long time waiting in my kitchen. The party went on till about five or six in the morning, and I don't mind telling you that Garbo enjoyed herself.

We played various games like charades and danced a lot and discussed all sorts of subjects right into the morning. One surprise remark of Garbo's I remember distinctly. 'You are all so gifted, here. I have nothing to offer you!'

For myself the party did me a lot of good. I went straight to the studio to have my face slapped by Laughton in the film *Devil and the Deep*. I went right through the day's work and never felt better in my life. I think it was the excitement that kept me going until five o'clock the following morning.

That was the last I saw of Garbo, but the memory of her will always remain in my mind as a most charming, vivid, colourful personality, genuinely shy, but a delightful companion when she knows you.

When you think that before Garbo went to America she could not speak a word of English, the work she has done on the talkies is really remarkable. She is a woman of great intelligence. She speaks German fluently and has a good sense of humour. I think she is the only artist who appeared on the silent screen who could make a success on the theatre stage. I should like to see her play Ibsen parts, and she told me that she would adore to do so. I doubt, however, if she could ever overcome her shyness enough.

To show that I am not exaggerating when I speak of the veneration that Hollywood has for Garbo, I will tell you the inside story of the Will Rogers-Wallace Beery hoax and the way it was received. At the premiere of *Grand Hotel* all the stars of Hollywood were expected to be present except Garbo, who never attends premieres.

Will Rogers, who was acting as M.C., announced that there would be a big surprise. Everybody waited in suspense for the surprise. Then, at the end of the picture Will Rogers announced that Garbo would make a personal appearance.

The excitement was intense, because Garbo had never done that before. Then came the anti-climax. Wallace Beery walked on dressed up as Garbo. There was not a hand. Nobody laughed. People were more inclined to cry, such was their disappointment.

A JOURNEY WITH KARENINA

Basil Rathbone

If Salka Viertel can be held in any degree responsible for having encouraged Garbo to make such a disappointing film as *The Painted Veil*, she immediately made amends by suggesting a remake of Tolstoy's classic story, *Anna Karenina*. The part of the tragic heroine was not new to Garbo because she had made a silent version of the same novel in 1927 with John Gilbert called *Love*. Salka again had a hand in the screenplay with S. N. Behrman who had produced such excellent dialogue for *Queen Christina*. Clarence Brown was the director yet again working in conjunction with cameraman William Daniels. The story of frustrated love set in nineteenth-century Russia was lavishly staged and superbly photographed, and the performances of the supporting actors – in particular the rapidly maturing young Basil Rathbone – made the finished picture enormously popular with critics and cinemagoers alike. In quick succession, *Anna Karenina* won Garbo the New York Film Critics Award for the best female performance of the year, and was judged the Best Foreign Film of the Year by the International Motion Picture Exposition held in Italy.

During the making of the film Basil Rathbone, like so many of his predecessors, fell under Garbo's spell and recorded his impression for *Film Weekly* in September 1936 as *Anna Karenina* began its worldwide release. Later Rathbone and his wife, Ouida, were to become friends with Garbo, and a favourite story of theirs recalled how she had once played a practical joke on them by attending one of their parties disguised as Prince Hamlet. It was not until the following day that the couple realised that the slim masked 'youth' in Shakespearean costume who had mingled almost unnoticed among their guests had been none other than the 'silent Swede' herself!

Basil Rathbone with Garbo in
Anna Karenina *(1935)*

221

first met Garbo in 1922. I used to go along to visit John Gilbert quite a lot, and Garbo and I were introduced at one of his parties. There was a jolly crowd present. Most of them were good-looking Hollywood stars. But there was no one there so radiantly beautiful as Garbo. I could look only at her eyes at first. They are indescribably lovely and expressive.

I sat next to her at lunch. She had no make-up on. I kept looking at her glorious hair – and those big eyes. There was nothing languorous about her. She was a great sport – and great fun. She played tennis energetically and really well. She swam beautifully.

Then, in 1931, I met her again. She had changed. Physically, she was still just as beautiful (I think she is even lovelier today). But her manner was detached. I met her again in Hollywood last year when I appeared with her in *Anna Karenina*. She had changed even more. I got the impression of someone in distress. All that jolliness had disappeared completely. Talking to her I felt somehow that I was intruding. She seemed to be tired.

The only explanation I can offer is that Garbo has inherently the spirit of her native land – Sweden – which is a great longing for being alone. Nowadays, it seems that she is never happier than when she is in her garden, or walking alone or with some very close friend. Please don't think, however, that she has lost any of her human appeal. She is still a woman whom one instinctively likes. One little incident will give you all the evidence you need to believe this.

Little Freddie Bartholomew who plays Anna Karenina's son, Sergei, and I became good friends. One morning, I noticed that he was not his usual self. He was obviously ill at ease. I asked him what was wrong.

'I have never met Miss Garbo, and I really am so frightened,' he confessed.

I told him not to worry, and that she was a very charming woman. So I took him along and introduced him to her. He put out his hand politely. 'How do you do, Miss Garbo?'

He spoke nervously. But within three minutes all his fears had disappeared, and in a short time Freddie had become tremendously fond of Miss Garbo. You can always trust a child's intuition.

Acting with Garbo is a delight. She has the art of film-making right at her fingertips. It is absolutely instinctive. I have said so before, and I repeat it now, that I learned more about picture-acting from her, simply by working with her, than from anyone else up to that time. She is a thoroughly 'economical' player. Everything she does or says on the screen means something. She never exaggerates a gesture or an expression.

Until *Karenina* I was never quite sure about screen acting. I was uneasy, not quite knowing how much to act or how much one could economise in movement and expression, as compared to the stage. But after playing with Garbo I knew. By watching her I learned everything I know about acting for the screen. She has this technique of economy raised to an art. She made tiny movements, minute changes of expression which I actually didn't notice at the time, but when I saw the scene on the screen I was amazed.

There was a scene in *Karenina*, for instance, where I had to tell her while we were out driving in a carriage that she was seeing too much of this other man, Vronsky. She said nothing and seemed to do nothing. But on the screen I found she had made a tiny movement, the slightest possible drawing away from me, so that she did not touch me as we sat. That little gesture could not have been more effective: it told the whole story. With it she conveyed an impression of utter loathing.

Sometimes now when I'm rehearsing a scene I think back to moments like that and wonder how Garbo would play it – or rather how little she would do.

225

Robert Taylor CAMILLE AND I

By the time *Anna Karenina* was made, Garbo was beyond dispute the most famous film actress alive. That most urbane of commentators, Alistair Cooke, described her as 'the unapproachable goddess of the most widespread and remarkable mythology in human history'. This mythology took many forms. Her looks, her hairstyles, her hats and clothes were slavishly imitated by women all over the world. Her likeness was painted by innumerable artists, and film makers everywhere vied with each other to find Garbo lookalikes for the screen. She was featured in stage plays and musical sketches, in parodies and even Walt Disney cartoons. Jingles extolling her peerless beauty and high-flown love songs like 'I Dreamed I was Kissed by Greta Garbo' poured from composers' pens. Her fan mail was gigantic, adoring letters by the thousands offered her the fortunes of lovesick millionaires and the hearts of penniless youths. She ignored them all, but still they poured into the MGM offices.

In 1937 Garbo gave what many people believe to be her finest screen performance in the title role of *Camille*. As the wayward and ultimately tragic Marguerite in this version of Alexandre Dumas' classic romance, she brought a depth of emotion and suffering to the part which far surpassed any previous performances and caused the film to be hailed as a masterpiece. The picture won the New York Film Critics Award, and Garbo was nominated for an Oscar. (It was won, though, by Luise Rainer for her role in Pearl Buck's *The Good Earth*.)

Some of the credit for the power and beauty of the picture must be accorded to the director George Cukor and Garbo's male lead, the fast rising young star Robert Taylor. Cukor — who will be giving his thoughts on Garbo in a later article — says that the actress adopted a rather unusual attitude towards Robert Taylor, who played her youthful lover, Armand. 'While we were making *Camille*,' he recalled, 'she spoke very little to him. She was polite, but distant. She had to tell herself that he was the ideal young man, and she knew if they became friendly, she'd learn he was just another nice kid.' Taylor himself, as he writes in the following article which appeared in a special *Picturegoer* supplement issued to mark the release of the film in Britain in September 1937, was not aware of any special attitude on Garbo's behalf, although he readily confesses to the debt he owed his co-star. The piece is also interesting for the information it provides on the preparation work that went into *Camille* as well as the actual filming.

Robert Taylor in a dramatic moment from **Camille** *(1937)*

It was in the spring of 1937 that preparations were begun for the new Greta Garbo picture, *Camille*, in which I was to have the honour of playing opposite her.

For those unfamiliar with the production of motion pictures, it should be said that the actual photography requires only about one-third of the time elapsing between the first discussions to select a story and delivery of the film to the theatre manager.

The classic romance of Marguerite and Armand which the younger Alexandre Dumas wrote eighty-four years ago, had been selected and the scenario department was at work on adapting the love story to the wider scope of the screen.

The screen has the advantage over the novel of sound and visible representation to make the story more real. Both stage and screen stories have a more difficult task indicating the thoughts of characters than is experienced in a novel, but the scenarists seem equal to it. And while the stage has a third dimension to its picture of reality, there is not the opportunity on the stage for emphasis of dramatic points through close-ups nor is it practical to shift stage scenes to produce the interesting variety of geographical background and point of view which on the screen make stories more effective.

When the writers have finished rephrasing the story so as to employ all the manifold advantages of the screen in telling it vividly, the designers under Cedric Gibbons start to work. The script is made available at the same time to the actors. I studied the character of Armand and the lines given me to make him come alive for many weeks before a scene was rehearsed before the camera.

Garbo with the director of Camille, *George Cukor*

Many revisions are made at this stage of a screenplay's

229

development. As did other players, I discussed my problems in the role of Armand with director George Cukor and members of the production staff and some slight changes resulted. Occasionally an idea set forth in the script is impractical, or can be improved. It makes no difference where a better idea comes from: it's used.

Accepted designs for sets are first built as models. With these miniatures, Cukor planned the action of the story, its varying tempo and mood. Cameraman Bill Daniels considered his lighting problems at the same time. It was much easier to discover necessary changes by planning with miniatures than it would have been to attempt to alter the completed sets for *Camille*.

With the advice of the research department, the property men meanwhile had been assembling decorations for the set. Edwin Willis had gone to Europe that summer to purchase beautiful antiques for *Camille*, and the effect he and his assistants created was exquisite. The construction department started its carpenters, glass-blowers, plasterers, painters and metal craftsmen at work to build the sets from the corrected designs and the drapers prepared to assemble the background for the actors as stage space became available.

Incidental music is composed and orchestrated at this time when the picture requires it. The *Camille* cast soon began conferences with Adrian over costumes he designed, and we stood for careful fittings as the wardrobe was completed. While the make-up men experimented with their effects, camera tests were made of the costumes.

All this complex activity is planned to be finished at the same time, and then the troupe assembles to make its first scene. When it is considered that a large number of productions are being made at once and that interruption of schedules may bring a head-on collision of two companies seeking to use the same stage space, it is apparent that operating such a studio as Metro-Goldwyn-Mayer presents a planning and dispatching problem worthy of the best minds.

When people talk of temperamental studio artists, I have to laugh. Artists they must be, of course, but they're of the most practical sort. I have always admired Miss Garbo and I was delighted to play opposite her. Sixteen other actors, and may I add that they were the most distinguished actors of the screen, had preceded me in romantic roles with this great star. I felt I had to do better

230

than I had ever done before if my work in *Camille* was to be compared with the acting of those who had already played Miss Garbo's lovers.

Throughout the weeks of preparations for *Camille*, I had never met Miss Garbo. I had never even seen her except on the screen. When I watched her in film plays, in fact, it was for the pleasure the show gave me, and I never dreamed I might have a personal interest in how love scenes with her could be presented. We did not meet until the first day of work in *Camille*. Our first set was the elaborately decorated interior of the Théâtre de Variétés as it existed in Paris in 1846. Fully a hundred other players in costumes of the period were gathered in groups around the big stage when I arrived. I was a stranger to all of them, so I waited at one side until somebody noticed me.

Scenes in which I didn't appear were shot for two hours. They were atmospheric pictures of gay groups moving through the theatre foyer, chatting and laughing. I just waited. George Cukor, the director, was in a huddle with his staff when Miss Garbo entered. None of them saw her and I had to look several times before I was sure it was she. The Garbo bob was gone and her hair fell in long curls to her shoulders. She was wearing grey slacks that became the slender grace with which she smilingly approached the group.

She greeted Bill Daniels, the cameraman whom she had known longest, and Porter, the electrician. Director Cukor then introduced the others of his staff and looked around for me. I walked over when he called, and I was presented.

'I am pleased to know you,' she said with a pleasant smile and I believe she meant it. I know I was thrilled to meet her. What a moment for a young actor who had risen from obscurity in just two years and was now to be the screen lover of the woman who had been the reigning queen of the screen for ten years!

A few minutes later, though, I was rehearsing my first scene with Miss Garbo. Ordinarily, this is a very nervous moment for any actor, yet I seemed to fall into my first scene with her without any sense of nervousness or strangeness. Naturally, I had nursed an anxiety for months to work in a picture with Miss Garbo, for I knew it would be the biggest picture in my life so far. But truthfully, I was not afraid of her. I was no more unnerved in playing my first scenes than I had been during the first scenes of any other picture that had gone before.

I knew she was Garbo. I understood the veil of glamour wrapped around her. I was aware that she is a great actress, undoubtedly the greatest, and an extraordinary personality. My first impressions of her, and they still remain with me, were that she is a very companionable and friendly person with whom to work. I felt exceedingly grateful for the privilege of working with her. But I had no fear of the lady, and I am sure Miss Garbo will appreciate my frankness in saying so.

One thing I did discover. She possesses a certain quality which no one can possibly learn from her, no matter how long he studies it. She has a great pair of eyes. In the scenes before the cameras, she seems to use her eyes so little. Yet, when those same eyes appear on the screen they reveal that they are constantly performing miracles of expression.

She works harder in her scenes than I could believe any artist could work. She is tireless and always so anxious to repeat the scene as often as necessary to reach perfection. Yet none of the scenes, no matter how often they are repeated, seem to satisfy her. I have never met a more natural woman than Miss Garbo, all other reports to the contrary. Much of the coldness that has been ascribed to her, I believe, has been caused by some reason outside of herself. Naturally, she is friendly. Naturally, she is anxious about her work and she is straightforward. I have never heard her condemn or disapprove. Instead, she will remark she is 'anxious' about it.

She is gifted with an absolutely uncanny craftsmanship, and she has a delightful sense of humour. As for her craftsmanship, before the first scene is shot she knows all her lines and all the lines of those who play opposite her. Her sense of humour was very evident throughout the filming of *Camille*. I have seen her ride the camera dolly around the set during the scenes in which she did not appear, just to enjoy a playful ride.

I also understand that on all previous pictures, music on the stage was taboo when Miss Garbo was working. This certainly was not so during the recent picture. She requested Mickey Whalen's orchestra to play several rumbas for her. She requested Rex Evans, one of the players, to play a few of her favourite pieces on the piano. As the picture progressed and as the more dramatic scenes approached, Miss Garbo felt she could play them better after listening to Negro spirituals on the set. The records were provided and it was upon my own electric gramo-

phone that the mood music was played. This mood music gave us one of our biggest laughs. While we were awaiting a camera and light set-up for a carriage shot on stage eleven, Miss Garbo, Laura Hope Crews and I broke into song – with a none-too-good rendition of 'Home, Home on the Range'. We had our little laugh, then settled down to work. Next day, Miss Garbo and I were back on stage four for one of the tensely dramatic scenes. For the rehearsal, Miss Garbo requested that a Negro spiritual be played. As we started our rehearsal, the loud speaker suddenly boomed forth with our strident execution – and I mean execution – of 'Home, Home on the Range'. Without our knowledge, director Cukor had had a wax record made of our playful prank of the day before. It was many long minutes before we could again get back into a dramatic mood.

Another fine trait of Miss Garbo's is that she has a deep sympathy for unfortunates. A stray dog wandered onto the set one day. Instead of having it ejected, Miss Garbo ordered food for the animal and permitted him to join our company for the rest of the day.

Shortly before Christmas a girl selling handkerchiefs entered the stage by mistake. As the officer on guard was leading her to the door, Miss Garbo asked the frightened youngster to her dressing room. When she emerged, the child's handkerchief box was empty. Miss Garbo had purchased the entire supply.

Not alone her fellow players, but all the directors who have worked with her swear by her. *Camille*, like many of her other pictures, had an unhappy ending. According to Mr Cukor, only Garbo's greatness permits her to star repeatedly in pictures with unhappy endings. There is no other actress, either of the stage or screen, Cukor told me, who has established herself in such a position of greatness that she can consistently return to her public in unhappy themes.

None but the great figures of the stage and screen can dare take the risk of jeopardising their careers so frequently with unhappy endings. Of the outstanding stars of the screen, Miss Garbo is the only one who dares do so. She is given this right because she holds the position in the film world that Mme Duse held in the theatre. She is best fitted for them because she is at her best in tensely dramatic roles that build up to stark tragedy. The unhappiness of her characterisations was inevitable, because it strengthened the dramatic tensity of the story.

I even venture to predict that even when Miss Garbo becomes a memory it is unlikely that another will reach the zenith in the art of acting that Miss Garbo possesses. Yet, I can truthfully say that Miss Garbo never once stole a scene. She gave all the members of her supporting cast the advantage of every opportunity that was presented to them. Naturally, she dominates any picture she is in, but she never does it deliberately. She never demands favours. If the scene belongs to another player he gets everything he deserves with her fullest co-operation. She takes direction very easily. Whatever the director demands, she responds whole-heartedly.

Wilhelm Sörensen THE STRANGEST HOLIDAY

It was perhaps only appropriate that the screen's most adored romantic actress should next play the role of a woman at the centre of one of history's most famous and ill-fated romances – that of Napoleon for the Polish Countess Marie Walweska, who legend claims was his favourite mistress. Great care, money and attention to detail was lavished on *Conquest*, with Clarence Brown brought in once again to direct, and the French heart-throb, Charles Boyer, cast as Napoleon. However, despite a script by Salka Viertel and S. N. Behrman and some quite stupendous action scenes of warfare, the picture proved a disappointment to critics and fans alike. There was a general feeling that Garbo's performance lacked vitality, John Mosher in *The New Yorker* summing up the concensus of opinions when he wrote, 'Madame Garbo's elegant anaemia, I fear, can pall a little. Her performance seems static, though the story covers a period of years. Beautiful, fragile, and tired, she stands in the first scene among the Cossacks invading her husband's house; and quite unchanged, fragile and tired still, she waves her last farewell to Napoleon, as though she would assert and try to prove that loyalty is but a symptom of exhaustion.' Was Garbo finally growing tired and disillusioned with her career, he and other observers wondered?

It has been suggested by more than one critic that the 'somnambulist' state into which Garbo had apparently fallen had been brought about not only by her disillusionment with certain of the film roles she had been given, but also because there was a vital element missing from her life – love. Though she still had her small circle of friends – they were just *friends*, though – much of her time was spent lonely and isolated at home. There was no special man in her life. That is until 1937 when she met Leopold Stokowski, one of the leading classical musicians in America, and for twenty-four years conductor of the Philadelphia Orchestra.

Though Stokowski with his striking appearance and mane of white hair was over twenty years older than Garbo, his vitality and energetic attentions towards her swept her into what was soon being described as a 'world-shaking romance'. The newspapers informed their eager readers that Garbo had, at last, found her 'dream man'. Stokowski, they said, had told Garbo that they were destined to have a great romance like that of Wagner and Cosima, and indeed before long they were being spotted together at social events and in fashionable restaurants. Cornered by journalists at a party, Garbo was forced to answer the most pressing of their questions. 'I will not deny that Mr Stokowski and I are very good

The 'languid' Garbo in **Conquest** *(1937)*

237

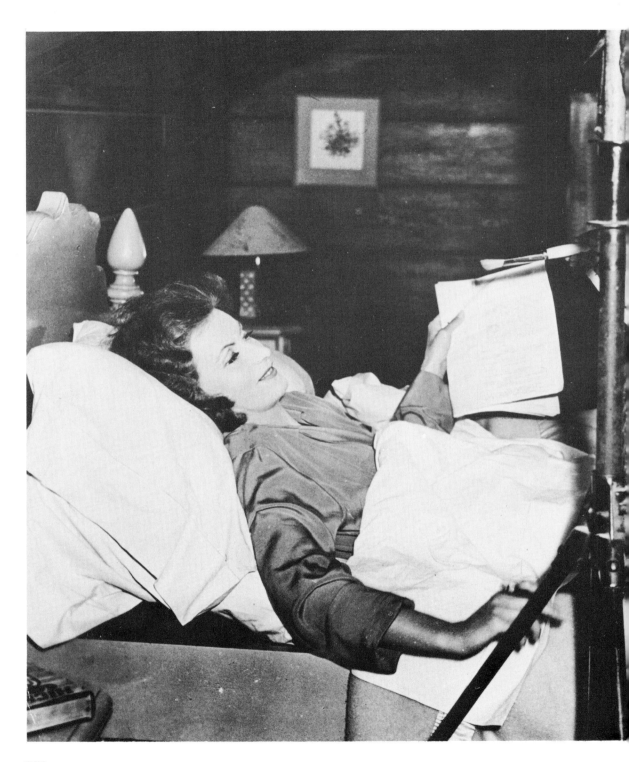

friends,' she said. 'But as far as marriage to him — no. That is out of the question.' At Christmas, Garbo returned home to Sweden once again to visit her relatives, while Stokowski finalised his divorce and then sailed to Italy.

In February, the ever-alert ears of the world's press heard that the couple had been reunited at a villa which Stokowski had hired in the tiny, historic village of Ravello overlooking the Mediterranean. Within hours, reporters were camped outside the Villa Cimbrone in droves creating a 'monstrous journalistic siege' to quote one eye-witness. The extraordinary events which followed their discovery — both what went on inside and outside the villa — how the couple were forced to flee across Europe and eventually found sanctuary briefly in Sweden, as well as the strange ending of the affair, are here described by one of the few people who were privy to what went on, Garbo's long-time confidant, Wilhelm Sörensen. His account, published in June 1955, in the *Sunday Express*, is surely the definitive statement on the most famous of Garbo's relationships after that with John Gilbert.

Garbo 'taking it easy' on the set of Two-Faced Woman *(1941)*

239

I helped Garbo in her successful search for seclusion when fame first burst upon her. Years later, in 1939 to be exact, she enlisted my aid once again. It was the time when she was making her much-publicised tour of the Continent with Leopold Stokowski, the grey-haired conductor. Was she in love with him? Were they going to marry? I honestly don't think so. From what I know about it, the tour was the most notorious – *and yet the most unromantic* – voyage *à deux* of all time.

They set out first of all for Capri, the honeymoon island in the Mediterranean. Reporters from all over the world immediately set up a day-and-night vigil around the villa where they were staying. They were convinced that Garbo had at last succumbed to the call of love and was about to say 'Yes' to a marriage proposal from the handsome musician who had persuaded her to leave America with him.

The world thought it was a palpitating romance. But, as Garbo was later to describe it to me, romance was the last thing that concerned these two travellers. Once more what she was concerned with was not love, but companionship. The two of them spent their time in Capri following a strict programme of exercise and diet. Early in the morning, Garbo would rout out Stokowski and get him on the balcony in his bathing costume to teach him Swedish exercises. She never learned to call him by any intimate name, so that when he made a mistake she would cry: 'No, no, no, Mister Stokowski. You are too slow. Like this, like this.'

She kept him on a vegetarian diet of carrots and salads. (She had never been so strict when she was with me.) She confused the servants by secreting food in her suitcase, which she did not allow Stokowski to see or use; and by

Clarence Brown directing Garbo and Charles Boyer on the set of Conquest

wolfing cakes and other starchy foods in the privacy of her room.

After three weeks of being besieged by the world Press, anxious to know if they were to be married, Garbo and Stokowski struck a bargain. In return for being left alone, they consented to Garbo giving an interview. She came into the lounge of the Villa Cimbrone, on Capri, looking pale and agitated. Her face was set and miserable.

'Well,' she said, challengingly, 'what do you want?'

She was asked if it were true that she was going to marry Stokowski. She shook her head, and again when someone asked if she were already married. Suddenly, as if she had to try to make clear her philosophy of life, her idea of human relationships, she added: 'There are some people who want to get married and there are others who do not. I never had any impulse to go to the altar.'

This attempt to satisfy the press proved of no avail, however, and when it became evident they would not be left in peace, the couple set off to roam the Continent. Garbo's tour with Stokowski came to a halt at her estate, Harby, which is located fairly close to Nyköping on the Baltic coast south of Stockholm. She had bought the estate, which consisted of a fifteen-room house and a thousand acres of land, some years previously, as a holiday haven.

I was then spending the summer on the west coast above Gothenburg. One day in early June I heard Garbo's voice on the telephone. 'Hello, Sören,' she said. 'What's this place Svinevik you told me about so many times. Is it still there?' (*Svinevik was the name of a summer villa on the shores of a fiord I had frequently raved about to Garbo as an ideal place for her vacation.*)

'Why do you ask?'

'Well, I'd like to live there for a while.'

I said: 'Greta, you should have called a week ago. I've just rented it out for the season.'

'Just my luck,' she sighed. 'Can't you fix it? Maybe the people who rented it can get another house.'

It was going to be difficult to annul the lease, since I had regularly let out Svinevik to the same family for several years running. But I did know of another house on the other side of the fiord. With the help of the local forester I managed to persuade the owner to let out his place. I exerted myself, for this was for Garbo – even though it was for Stokowski, too.

Everything was finally arranged. But my labours proved

to be in vain. I was informed by telephone that Garbo and Stokowski had had an automobile accident between Nyköping and Stockholm. The maestro had suffered such a severe shock that he did not dare to venture on any more extended automobile trips in Sweden.

Indeed, he abruptly decided to cut his trip with Garbo short. The reason for it I shall never know. She did not talk to me about it. Nor, so far as I know, to anyone. But suddenly, in July, Stokowski left by himself to return to New York.

Garbo telephoned me. 'Stokowski has gone,' she said. 'I too will soon be going back to America, but before I do I'd like to ask you a favour. I've never seen the first film I played in – the film that's meant more to me than any other – *Gösta Berling's Saga*. Can you arrange for me to see it privately – just for me alone?'

After a bit of wangling I fixed it. I immediately called Garbo, and she made a date, and added in her happiest voice: 'I hope you have a nice dark suit handy, because if you do you'll be invited to dinner after the show.'

I was so excited by what she had said that I sent for a bottle of champagne and started drinking it. The doorbell rang and when I opened it there were two women standing outside. But no, I was not seeing double – Garbo had brought a friend with her, the Countess Wachtmeister. Garbo was wearing a heavy overcoat and slacks, and a trilby hat. It was an indescribable combination. She swept off her hat and bowed before me and kissed my hand.

She was either very nervous or as intoxicated as I was. This was the first time we had seen each other for many, many months. Countess Wachtmeister and I remained outside the cinema while Garbo watched her film. When she emerged, she looked emotionally drained. Was it the aftermath of the Stokowski affair – or the reunion with me? I certainly hadn't the heart to interject what would only have been irrelevant remarks. Garbo merely said that she looked forward to seeing us later that evening, and left the office by herself.

At eight o'clock I showed up for dinner in what I hoped was a presentable dark suit. Garbo was at the Stockholm apartment of Countess Wachtmeister and I thought that was where we would spend the evening. But I hadn't reckoned with Garbo's mysterious ways. A few minutes later the three of us left in a taxi, which took us to the fashionable home of the Wenner-Grens.

Mrs Marguerite Wenner-Gren was both host and hostess, since her famous financier-husband was off in some part of the world, presumably concluding a new business deal of international importance. In a dining room gleaming with silver and bronze we were served one superb dish after the other; Garbo, however, concentrated most of her attention on our hostess's lap, which was occupied by Chihuahuas, the world's smallest type of dog. At regular intervals the Madame would feed them a slice of partridge or any of the other delicacies that were near at hand.

'Just think, Sören.' Garbo whispered to me disapprovingly as we clinked our glasses across the table in a champagne toast.

The Napoleon love story was also known as Marie Walewska, *as this souvenir magazine proves*

After dinner we went 'sightseeing', which is probably the best word to describe our hurried, businesslike tour through the many rooms of that house. With hands clasped behind her back, Garbo followed her hostess like a faithful American tourist, seemingly intent on not missing a thing.

'This is my best Goya,' said Mrs Wenner-Gren, pointing to a magnificent painting bathed in special illumination. Whereupon Garbo piped up in a voice that the countess and I distinctly heard: 'Gosh, do we have to look at more – "goja" – now?' 'Goja' is also Swedish slang for 'rubbish'.

With the completion of the sightseeing tour the problem then arose how to make the evening pass entertainingly. That gave Garbo a brilliant idea: 'Mrs Wenner-Gren, isn't your yacht anchored out in the harbour now? I would just love to go on board.'

A splendid suggestion thought Mrs Wenner-Gren, who immediately put through a call to the yacht by direct telephone. Within the hour Garbo, Countess Wachtmeister, Mrs Wenner-Gren and I were on our way towards the yacht.

It was gaily illuminated with a garland of lights, and most of the crew were manning the bulwarks as we climbed on board. We did another sightseeing tour, topped off by more bottles of champagne. Just before breaking-up time Mrs Wenner-Gren distributed small gifts to each of her guests. I was given a couple of Siamese silver cuff-links with elephant insignia, the kind which presumed a world of patience on the part of the owner. Garbo received a beautiful crystal ampoule made by one of the leading perfume manufacturers.

When we set foot on dry land once again Garbo asked me what I'd been given. I obediently showed her the cuff links. Without a word she thrust the perfume bottle into my hand and said peremptorily: 'All right, let's change!'

That's the last I ever saw of those cuff links!

In due course I asked her what she had thought of our evening. Her answer was: 'Well, under no circumstances would I want to live like that!' But of Stokowski she did not mention one word.

George Cukor directing Garbo in Two-Faced Woman *(1941)*

THE CRAFT OF GARBO

George Cukor

If Garbo returned to Hollywood in a somewhat lighter mood than she had left it nine months before, she immediately had a chance to express this feeling in her next film, *Ninotchka*. Although she was known to audiences everywhere as the great romantic tragedienne, she had often felt the urge to play a comedy role – although the idea had appalled her studio. Now, though, she was given the chance (for what reasons we cannot be quite sure, except in a possible attempt to broaden her appeal still further) and she proved she had a sure touch of humour in the story of a Russian lady commissar dispatched to Paris to sort out some erring comrades and instead falling in love with a playboy played by Melvyn Douglas. A highlight of the story was Garbo drunk on champagne giggling like a schoolgirl. This was a moment for every Garbo fan to savour: a moment of screen history. The aloof, enigmatic face that had previously usually signalled emotion through the eyes with scarcely a facial movement, now shone with laughter. It was a sight no audience had seen before, an emotion only those close to Garbo were aware she actually possessed in abundance when the mood was right.

Naturally enough MGM publicised the picture quite simply with the words, 'GARBO LAUGHS!' And the combination of this intriguing element plus the fact it was well directed (by Ernst Lubitsch), finely scripted (by Charles Brackett, Billy Wilder and Walter Reisch) and stylishly photographed (William Daniels as ever), made *Ninotchka* a critical and box office success. The *New York Herald-Tribune* declared that 'the great actress reveals a command of comic inflection which fully matches the emotional depth or tragic power of her earlier triumphs', and once again she was nominated for an Oscar. (Once more, though, she was pipped at the post by Vivien Leigh in *Gone With The Wind*.) But the high spirits of the film did not carry on long for Garbo. The Second World War had broken out and although it seemed a long way off to Americans, it was to have far reaching effects for Garbo, as John Bainbridge has written: 'Her career was more seriously affected by the spreading war than that of probably any other Hollywood actress because her pictures had always earned more money abroad than in the United States. In fact few, if any, Garbo films ever returned their investment from exhibition in the United States alone.' It was not surprising, therefore, that when MGM came to contemplate her next film, they should try and tailor something that would appeal to the home market now that war-torn Europe was being denied to them.

The choice was *Two-Faced Woman*. A rather insubstantial tale about a plain wife who wins back her indifferent husband by impersonating her own beautiful twin sister and having an affair with him. From this MGM hoped a 'new Garbo' would emerge and they engaged the trusty Salka Viertel and S. N. Behrman for the script, Melvyn Douglas again as her co-star, and as director, George Cukor, who had made the triumphant, *Camille*. One might reasonably have expected that such an assembly of talents would have been able to make gold from even such an inauspicious plot: but, sadly, the result was a failure. Garbo, her hair bobbed, throwing herself into a new dance routine *and* appearing in a swimming costume for the first time was just not what the public expected. Nor was it something the National Legion of Decency could accept, and they condemned the picture for its 'immoral and un-Christian attitude towards marriage and its obligations; impudently suggestive scenes, dialogue and situations; and suggestive costumes'. Garbo was horrified at this reaction, and MGM took hasty action, shooting some new footage which intimated that the husband had known what was happening all along. The critics greeted the revised version with even less pleasure than the first, all agreeing that it was a totally absurd vehicle for Garbo. 'It is almost as shocking,' *Time* magazine said, 'as seeing your mother drunk.' And when Garbo uttered her last line in the picture, 'In this harsh new world there is no place for me anymore,' they were to prove more prophetic words than even she could have realised at the time.

George Cukor, the widely admired director who during his career earned the reputation of being able to handle even the most temperamental female stars, has spoken of his work with Garbo in what was to prove the finale of her screen career. In the following comments given in an interview with *Photoplay* in April 1972 he talks first about life at MGM in the 1930s and then his feelings on *Camille* and *Two-Faced Woman*. As the last director to have worked with Garbo his words have a special poignancy about them.

Garbo laughs at herself – a clever still for **Ninotchka** *(1939)*

249

There are all sorts of very authoritative-sounding books about how it was at MGM in the thirties, written by people who were *not* there. There is this cliché to be found in all their writings: 'Oh, how could you live in that factory? How awful it was! You had no freedom of expression. They were crass and commercial. *Nowadays*, we can express ourselves with no restraints.'

Well, I would like to say something *for* the studio system – and I was not a company boy. I think the producers and studio executives were very smart showmen. They provided you with all kinds of things. You could have the best stories, the best actors, the best technicians, the best scripts. You were helped enormously all along the way in making films. Also there were intelligent restraints. People were not allowed to indulge themselves. A director couldn't say to a producer, 'Get out of here! I'm going to do this my way! I don't want to see you at all!' I think those relationships with the top people at MGM whom you respected were very salutary.

That's all gone now, of course. It's in the past – it'll never happen again. But I do want to emphasise that when people think about the studio system they should realise it was *not* a prison system. It was not full of buttonhole makers, people who didn't know anything, who crushed artists into the ground. That was not the case. It was tough, but certainly no tougher than it is now. I worked with those tycoons, and if you had anything at all to give they encouraged you. Why? Because it was to their advantage. They realised that talent was the coin of the realm and they were very sympathetic to it. Nowadays, I find it's a little too opportunistic. 'You're a genius,' someone will declare, 'You're wonderful.' And then if things don't go well, you're thrown to the dogs.

As a director I have long believed you have got to be on the level with the star, making him or her realise that you are looking out for their interests as well as your own – even if you have to be unflattering sometimes. I never row with people. Somewhere along the line I try to find a basis of mutual respect and benefit. I must be sympathetic, and I do give in to them on certain things. Cajolery and kidding and bullying are necessary, but the trick is to sense when to use them. You've probably noticed, especially at parties, that nobody can put on the old la-de-da business like actors and actresses. Dukes and duchesses just aren't in it with them. It may sound fatuous, but they're a good deal like children pretending to be grand. They not only weren't born to the purple; many of them came from especially obscure beginnings. So sometimes to get along with them it's necessary to reduce them to what they were. I remember saying to one actress, 'Now, honey, be reasonable or you'll wake up and find yourself giving those piano lessons again!' It jolted her, but she took it in good spirit, realising that she wasn't going to get by with anything.

Most of the supposedly difficult people check their unreasonable moods at the sound-stage door when they come to work. Any actress worthy of the name knows she isn't going to bluff or overawe her director, so she is not likely to jeopardise her picture by trying to. How she behaves off the set, of course, is her own business. I learned all about actresses on Broadway, directing the firebrand Jeanne Eagels, the outspoken Ethel Barrymore and the impulsive Ina Claire long before I got to Hollywood. I realised then that we all got on best if I made them feel good. Like anyone else, when they feel better, women behave better: they'll sing and dance for you. Women are realistic, they have a great deal of sense. Tell them the truth, never predict. Never tell them, for instance, that if they continue to behave in a certain way – like drinking too much for instance – their looks will deteriorate. That is forecasting and women don't want forecasting.

They will respond to any suggestion you make if it seems to make sense – but if you don't deliver, then watch out. I am a bit of a lion tamer really, but I know when to encourage. It is not a contest between us, but a collaboration. Every star requires different handling, of course. The first day or two on the production is a kind of 'settling-in'

A dispirited-looking Garbo on what was to prove her last film, Two-Faced Woman *(1941)*

252

period, during which I have to find out the technique that is going to work best. Which brings me to Greta Garbo. When I first met her to discuss *Camille*, I sensed that she was a little distrustful of me. Having her own ideas of how *La Dame aux Camellias* ought to be played on the screen, she was not unnaturally afraid we might clash. She was diffident with new people, but once she had decided she liked me, she admitted me to her friendship, gave me her confidence and offered the fullest co-operation in her work.

I never told her how to play a scene. First, I let her rehearse it the way she thought it ought to be done. Then I made suggestions of my conception of the scene, and we blended our ideas. If I had told her what to do she would have done it – but I would have lost something valuable, for she always had some fresh idea to offer. In her acting, she was the most practical craftswoman in the studio. She could play an intimate, tender scene apparently with all her concentration on the emotion of it, yet she was cleverly controlling her movements in relation to the camera and the lighting. It was positively amazing the way she used to go to the camera and, in a couple of shots, capture exactly what was required of her. If, however, something went wrong, and she hadn't got the scene right after the first half-dozen takes, she would go to pieces. She seemed to feel that all the inspiration had evaporated and her acting then became curiously awkward and amateurish. The only thing to do in those circumstances was to stop work and come back to it in the morning.

I think the key to Garbo's performance in *Camille* was her ability to suggest that she was dying of some fatal disease. When you first saw her she had this little, dry cough, and she'd clear her throat. You knew something was wrong because she was such an imaginative actress. There was one scene where she had difficulty catching her breath, but she was very discreet about the whole thing. She suggested that with her own personality, and she did it with taste.

Garbo was a very original actress altogether. She moved beautifully, and there were certain things she did – like they way she sank to her knees – things she could do that no other actress could. But how to get her emotions out? I didn't have to tell her sad stories. But you created an atmosphere where she was prepared to do it. You didn't do it cold. You sat down and said, 'Come on, dear, here's the scene, I think you maybe talk a little, not too much,' but you prepared the thing so there was a very sympathetic atmosphere.

Before he died, Irving Thalberg saw a couple of days' rushes for the film and said, 'She's awfully good, she's never been this good.' But I said, 'Irving, she's just sitting there.' And he replied, 'But she is relaxed, she's open.' There was a kind of gaiety in that particular performance, a kind of unguarded quality that is missing from a great many of her other performances.

She was a very subtle actress, able with a slight gesture to be enormously suggestive. Often she was the aggressor in love making, you know, reaching for the man first. A love scene has to be a *scene*. Very often film-makers don't realise that today. It's all so exhibitionistic and pointless, really. There was something I always found very erotic in *Camille* – the scene where Garbo leaves the table at the party. It was so original the way she did it – that sort of hot

impatience she and Armand had for each other. If you noticed, what was erotic was the way she leaned over him. Her body didn't touch his, but she gave him small kisses all around the face. It was so extraordinary!

On the set Garbo was not only very amenable, but really very comic. I remember once we were doing a particularly dry scene and I heard her refer to it as 'government business'. When I asked her what she meant, she replied, 'That is what I call dull scenes, they are like government business!'

Garbo always went through a great deal to get a scene right, and I said to her once that she seemed to act a role so easily. She laughed, and said that she would kill me for saying such a thing! You have to know how much to rehearse and not overdo it, so that the finished performance in the film will look spontaneous. Garbo knew how to do this.

I directed her last picture, of course. *Two-Faced Woman* was a novel idea – getting her to play twins – but we started shooting before the script was really finished. We went along as best we could, but the picture was bad.

Garbo and I were, and still are, great friends. She's very reticent, secretive, but has enormous charm. She's witty in her own way, but a lot of the jokes she makes are a sort of smoke screen, so that you don't get too close to her. She's a creature of the greatest distinction. She likes people . . . but only one at a time. She hasn't a lot of vitality and too many people worry her.

She was unique as an actress – a person born for the screen. She knew when to quit, she just sensed it. And she was much too intelligent ever to want to try and make a comeback.

DeWitt Bodeen MEMORIES OF GARBO

After completing *Two-Faced Woman*, Garbo left the MGM studios never to return. It was the end of her film career – but only the beginning of the far longer part of her life as a recluse, an enigma, an enduring legend preserved for ever on the light and shadow of film stock.

The Garbo legend has, of course, been sustained over the years in numerous ways. Those alive at the time her movies first appeared have continued to enthuse over them to each succeeding generation – and these generations have, in turn, found something enduring, magical and wholly fascinating about the pictures whenever they are reshown at special festivals or on television. Critics and biographers alike have studied her life and work with painstaking care – yet the mystique at the heart of all this – Garbo herself – has proved as elusive to pin down as ever. Every Garbo fan has, though, his or her own particular vision of this great lady of the screen, I think, and all the continuing flood of words and pictures do is to conjure up in their minds some familiar image from one cinematic moment or another. As with all legends, there have been those people who would deny it; who have found her acting dated, stylised, listless; her personality neurotic, self-centred, even megalomaniac. And as no human being is flawless, only the most obsessive fan would argue that there are not elements of truth in such claims. Because, really, could anyone have experienced the adulation which so quickly enveloped the shy, unsophisticated Greta Gustafsson and remain unaffected? Yet this is not the place for psychoanalysis, but rather the point to complete our study by reflecting on the lasting nature of her legend through the years that followed her last film.

'Memories of Garbo' is a fascinating appraisal of these years, and was written by a fan-turned-Hollywood screenwriter, DeWitt Bodeen for *Focus on Film*, in the summer of 1973. Bodeen was just sixteen when he discovered Garbo in her first American film, *The Torrent*. 'She was the most wonderful image I'd ever seen,' he confesses, and this began a love affair with 'the face of the century' which neither time or changing fashions have been able to alter. His essay reflects the feelings of many Garbo admirers I believe, as well as explaining something of her screen longevity. Perhaps most importantly of all it helps reinforce what I believe to be already self-evident: that the legend of Garbo will last well beyond the twentieth century. Indeed, as long as films are part of our culture there will be a place among the most important and influential of these for the very best pictures of the one and only Garbo.

The mystery lives on – Garbo in The Kiss *(1929)*

257

At the most, there are no more than a half-dozen movie stars who have become legends in their own time. The Queen of them all – 'La Divina', as she is known in Europe – remains the one and only Garbo.

Nearly thirty-five years have gone by since she made a film, yet she is still the best copy of all screen celebrities, and the re-releases of her MGM films have made her the only movie actress whose name by itself spells instant box-office.

In the last decade, the top ten money-makers picked every year by American exhibitors include names that are almost exclusively male; in some years, one actress – Elizabeth Taylor, Joanne Woodward, Doris Day, Julie Andrews, Ali McGraw, or Barbra Streisand – is numbered among the chosen ten; but almost every exhibitor will admit that if stars of revivals were eligible for the list, Garbo's name, above all other actresses, would be there regularly. An ironic admission, because during the years when she was acting, while she was always among the favoured international few, she rarely made the exclusively American top-ten lists. She makes them now, by proxy as it were, even though American audiences are no longer responsive to the star image of the actress. Thus for today's worldwide audience, Garbo is up there with the men of the hour – John Wayne, Clint Eastwood, Paul Newman, Marlon Brando, Steve McQueen.

Whenever the current release product lags or does not attract, an exhibitor books a season of Garbo films, and her lovely face saves his. It started in London one spring not so long ago when a Chelsea cinema booked a Garbo season. Crowds queued in lines around the block. Subsequently, a West End revival of her films in a larger house

A pose which few modern sex symbols could better – Garbo in the Twenties

259

brought out longer lines. Movie managers in the bigger American cities tried the same experiment starting in the late fifties, and I well remember standing then in line to see *Camille* at the Beverly Canon in Beverly Hills with a friend who had never seen a Garbo film. I had already stopped counting the number of times I'd seen Garbo as the Lady of the Camellias because after the fiftieth occasion, those who knew were looking at me as if I were some kind of religious fanatic. I still am, I suppose, about Garbo, because I think I've now seen *Camille* a good twenty-five times more.

When the Museum of Modern Art, several years ago in Manhattan, scheduled a festival of all her films, both foreign and American (except for *The Divine Woman* of which MGM says the negative has disintegrated and all prints are lost), tickets were sold out two days after they went on sale, and the programme was immediately scheduled for repetition.

She is a great favourite among the younger set, who know her from seeing revivals of her films both in cinemas and on television. The common query of today's teenager to an adult is 'I knew Garbo was beautiful, but why didn't you tell me what a marvellous actress she is?'

Just last autumn, when I was living in Spain, Spanish television showed all the MGM films of Garbo, silent and sound (except, of course, for *The Divine Woman*), and television viewing soared on the twice-weekly nights when her pictures were shown. All the top Spanish weeklies ran articles about her – '¡Hola!' 'Lecturas', 'Gaceta Ilustrada', and the very magazine that owes its name, 'Garbo', to her – and all were quick sell-outs at the news-stands. 'Gaceta Ilustrada' indicated that their issue, the tenth time they had featured a Garbo article since 1957, was, like the other nine, a collector's item before it came out.

Twelve years ago, when I was in Vienna, I remember seeing *Camille* and then, on another afternoon, *Conquest* (known as *Marie Walewska* in both Europe and England). It was something of a shock at first, because both pictures had been dubbed into German, and a voice other than Garbo's was speaking the lines in German of Marguerite Gautier and Marie Walewska. The packed house, two-thirds of whom were young, was enthralled, and when the house lights came up, viewers remained in their seats for a few moments to wipe the tears from their eyes. One young girl was weeping uncontrollably, and her companions clung to her, weeping with her. I myself was moved, even though the voice I'd heard was not Garbo's.

And then I remembered how it was when I first saw Garbo on the screen. The appeal then was purely visual, because the movies had not found their voice, and missing then were the low, thrilling, bemused tones of the actress. But there was the face, which has been called 'the face of the century', a face which, like Helen's, could have launched a thousand ships and topped many a topless tower. It was 1926, and although I was a senior at Fresno High School in Fresno, California, I had cut classes to catch the first matinee of a new MGM film, *The Torrent*, from the novel by Ibáñez. I don't know why I was attracted to that particular picture, but for the next three days, while *The Torrent* was playing the Kinema Theatre, nobody saw me. I spent afternoons and nights at the Kinema, because up there on the screen was an actress named Greta Garbo who was the most wonderful image I'd ever seen. I was glad when I learned she had come from Sweden, because I'm half Swedish, and felt a closer affinity.

I always read Robert E. Sherwood in those days, when he was reviewing films for the old weekly 'Life', and when he called Garbo a 'goddess' and the 'dream princess of his department', I entirely concurred. It was after seeing Garbo in her second MGM feature, *The Temptress* that Mr Sherwood wrote: 'I want to go on record as saying that Greta Garbo in *The Temptress* knocked me for a loop . . . [She] qualifies herewith as the official Dream Princess of the Silent Drama Department of "Life".' Two years later, Mr Sherwood was reviewing *The Mysterious Lady*, and Garbo had become his 'dream princess of eternity – the knockout of the ages'. I was of the same persuasion.

I was at Fresno State College when I saw her third film *Flesh and the Devil*. I was writing for the paper, and was given *Ben-Hur* to review, an assignment which ordinarily would have delighted me as it was the biggest prize of the season. But then I found that *Flesh and the Devil*, opening the same time at another theatre, had been handed to somebody I'd thought was a good friend. To my horror, he didn't like the picture and said so, and, what's worse, he liked the ingenue Barbara Kent better than Garbo. *Barbara Kent*? After that, I didn't like him. From that point on, there was nothing but a cool indifference between us, and ever since then, the very few I've known who are not Garbo worshippers I've dismissed as either trying to attract attention by being different, or as just having no taste whatsoever.

Soon thereafter I was in Los Angeles, a student at UCLA. Whatever I did, wherever I was, then and in all the years to come, Garbo remained the serene goddess, and whenever a new picture of hers opened, I abandoned whatever I was doing or studying to pay homage to the faraway princess.

Actually, she wasn't so far away. She was filming at MGM's studios in Culver City, living at numerous resident addresses in Santa Monica on San Vicente or Chevy Chase, or on Linden Drive in Beverly Hills (although that, I think, was actually her brother Sven's residence – her sister Alva died in Stockholm while Garbo was filming *The Temptress*). I began to see her, always alone, being driven to work early in the morning, and once when I was staying in Santa Monica for a weekend and took a midnight walk along the beach (one could walk alone there in those days at any hour with no fear of being hit over the head), coming toward me, walking barefooted in the wet sand, was Garbo, alone and perfectly content. She didn't look my way, and I looked the other way as we passed for fear she'd think I was staring – which I was.

I saw her again one night shortly afterward at the Shrine Auditorium during the annual opera season. It was for a performance, as I remember, of Strauss' 'Salome', and Jeritza was singing. Suddenly, as I lingered in the foyer, there came Garbo, head lowered, walking quickly, one hand on the arm of her manager, Harry Edington (the only manager she ever had). Years later, when I was working on a script at RKO for Edington* – (*Walk Away from 'Em*, which never got produced), I recalled that evening to Edington and he smiled.

'Yes,' he said, 'I remember that night when I took her to the opera. She had actually expressed a desire to go, and then at the last minute almost bowed out because she didn't have anything in her own wardrobe elegant enough to wear. I phoned the studio and MGM wardrobe lent her an evening dress and a wrap for the occasion. Even then, she was so self-effacing and there were so many other stars present that night who wanted to be photographed that I think few recognised her and no photographer, to my knowledge, tried to steal a shot of her.'

* Ironically, Harry Edington by this time had become the husband of that ingenue I had once termed the least likely to succeed, Barbara Kent.

Meanwhile, I'd caught her appearances in two major European films which were shown to enthusiastic foreign film audiences in Hollywood – as the lovely Italian bride in love with the dissolute man of God in the Swedish, Stiller-directed *Gösta Berling's Saga*; and in Pabst's German-made film, *The Joyless Street*, as the Viennese girl from a good family who is forced through circumstances to enter what was once called 'a house of assignation', where her first client is the young man she loves.

During those last few years of the silent film, which I sometimes cherish as the best in motion picture making, the films Garbo made are all filled with unforgettable moments: the youthful, laughing love scene on the floor between her and Lars Hanson in *The Divine Woman*; the tender scenes between her and the young Philippe De Lacy, playing her son, in *Love*, as well as the impassioned ones between her as Anna and John Gilbert as Vronsky in the same picture; the suspenseful moment in *The Mysterious Lady*, when she, a spy, kills her enemy, Gustav von Seyffertitz, and then, when a servant enters the room, sits on the dead man's knee and pretends to be his favourite for the evening as she signals to the servant to leave them alone; the scene of dismay when she learns in *The Single Standard* that Nils Asther, her lover with whom she is enjoying a yachting cruise, has dismissed her from his life and she distractedly but thoughtfully begins to wash her hair; the impassioned love scene in *A Woman of Affairs* when she gives herself to Gilbert and lets the loose ring slip from her finger, and again in the final reel when the bitter truth of her gallant lie is exposed and she turns up the death card in a solitaire pack and says via subtitle, 'You've taken from me the only decent thing I ever did', before going out to her death; the strange attraction she feels in *Wild Orchids* drawing her to the handsome but half-barbaric oriental prince, Nils Asther, when she has become resignedly happy with her elderly husband, Lewis Stone; and, finally, in her last silent, *The Kiss*, when she is on trial for murdering her insanely jealous husband and the defiant dignity she evinces when being defended by the attorney, Conrad Nagel, who loves her.

The talkies came, and gradually even the last three big hold-outs – Chaney, Garbo, and Chaplin – spoke. GARBO TALKS, all the choice twenty-four sheets in town announced, and it was an electric moment in *Anna Christie* when she makes her entrance after the first reel of preparation and finally, with deliberate calculation, speaks her

Overleaf: Susan Lennox: Her Fall and Rise *(1931)*

263

first lines in that wonderful husky voice: 'Whisky – ginger ale on the side – and don't be stingy with the whisky, baby'.

Thereafter in most of her other talking features only her very presence illuminated her films. It's especially true of *Romance*, in which she is stunningly photographed and gowned, but even in 1930 it was a creaky vehicle. Recently, on revisiting her third talking picture *Inspiration*, which I had not remembered as being as good as it is, I was pleased to note that the screenplay, suggested as it is by that old warhorse of the French theatre, Daudet's 'Sapho', is well constructed and the dialogue has real charm and sophistication. Gene Markey did his homework well on this one; but on the other hand, *As You Desire Me*, which I had remembered fondly (and it also has a Markey script), seems poorly directed, with hackneyed dialogue and unbelievable scenes, plus some very bad performances by some very good actors. And, again, it's only Garbo as the Pirandello heroine who lights up the screen with her own special incandescence.

Four other features from the talking era are most unworthy of her; *Susan Lennox: Her Fall and Rise, Mata Hari, The Painted Veil,* and her last – the clumsy, embarrassing *Two-Faced Woman*.

To the role of the fading ballerina, Grusinskaya, in *Grand Hotel*, for which she was actually more than a little miscast, Garbo brought a nervous, restless quality that somehow made Grusinskaya's dilemma very real, and her love scenes with John Barrymore are some of the best she ever played. They had great admiration for one another as fellow artists, and the sincerity came through abundantly.

The three near-perfect and two perfect Garbo talking features are *Queen Christina, Anna Karenina,* and *Conquest* on the one hand; and *Camille* and *Ninotchka* at the peak. She herself is wonderfully moving and believable as Sweden's unhappy Queen Christina; Rouben Mamoulian's direction of the somewhat artificial story often transcends the manufactured plot; and the two big silent moments with Garbo are unforgettable: when she memorises the room wherein she has loved for a night; and at the end, when her lover is slain and the sails of the ship are unfurled while she goes to the prow and remains staring out like a beautiful ship's figurehead, not moving a muscle of her exquisite face while the camera slowly moves in for what is without doubt her most glorious close-up. Every viewer of those final moments has his own

translation of what she is feeling, what she is thinking – it is perfect abstraction on film – and that is precisely the way Mamoulian wanted it.

Several years ago, when I was one of a chosen few who picked scenes from films of the past for a three-hour programme called 'The Movies' shown at a midnight viewing for those attending the live and film benefit show for the Motion Picture Relief Fund (it had three subsequent showings for Academy members at the Academy Award Theatre, which came off magnificently), these scenes from *Queen Christina* were chosen to represent Garbo. Mamoulian one Sunday afternoon brought two cans of film containing the only filmed tests Garbo is ever known to have made. One of them, Mr Mamoulian knew, had decomposed and could not be shown; it turned out to be the test Garbo had made with Laurence Olivier, who almost got the part until it was decided he photographed too young for her – and at her insistence John Gilbert was then engaged to play the Spanish lover. It would have been interesting to see Olivier with her, because Gilbert's performance is still regrettably the only weak one in *Christina*. The other reel, however, was in good condition, and was a silent wardrobe test, mostly of Garbo in the costumes she wore when she masqueraded as the young man, since these Adrian-designed clothes had to be exactly right. Garbo turned obligingly, putting on and taking off hats with just the right swagger or trying on capes, while that bemused smile lighted her eyes, framed as they were, and still are, with those incredible, naturally long lashes that curl down upon her cheeks like miniature ski-runs.

The talking version of *Anna Karenina* is especially interesting when seen as a companion piece to *Love*, its silent counterpart. There are moments in the modern-styled silent version which top those same episodes in the talking version. Garbo was always tremendously moving when she played scenes with children, and her scenes with young Freddie Bartholomew as her son are just as memorable as they had been previously in the silent version when she played them with Philippe De Lacy. As the silent Vronsky, Gilbert is more in the picture as a dashing lover than is the talking Fredric March, who seems to be busy acting in this one. Better in the talking version, however, is the final moment at the train station, when Garbo throws herself under the wheels of the train. David O. Selznick wanted in this scene that same mystic imperturbability which Mamoulian got from her. He had his then-assistant Val Lewton select a single frame of Garbo's best close-up as she stands watching the train. Over this close up projected continuously on a screen, the lights of the passing train flash and the sounds of the engine and the wheels of the cars on the track are all that is heard. And then the sad, forsaken, enigmatic face is obscured, and the passing lights, the steam, the sound rise, while the train itself disappears.

Camille remains the only movie I've ever seen where the audiences, no matter how many times they've seen it, always react as if they were at a live performance. When a sequence finishes and the fade-out begins, there is spontaneous applause just as there would be in a theatre when the curtain falls on a scene. *Camille* is a film which represents a meeting of talents that were perfect for its interpretation, and although it is beautifully cinematic, it is also soundly theatrical. It plays with effortless ease, like the well-made vehicle it is.

One of my favourite scenes is where Garbo, having made a rendezvous with Robert Taylor for late supper in her apartment is suddenly surprised by the unexpected return of Henry Daniell, her baronial lover. It was an added scene, and Daniell told me once how, on the morning he was to shoot it, he crossed the lot to his dressing-room and encountered Garbo on the way to hers.

She smiled wanly. 'How do you like the new scene, Mr Daniell?' she asked.

'I think it's a good scene,' he said cautiously, 'but I'm honestly worried about it. You see, I don't laugh very well.'

'I don't either,' she confessed plaintively.

That, of course, was the whole point of the scene and Cukor staged it with an electric brilliance.

Ninotchka was billboarded everywhere with two words – GARBO LAUGHS. MGM had tried a campaign on *Camille* with a catchphrase GARBO LOVES ROBERT TAYLOR, which was too much like school kids writing on a board fence. It didn't catch on as GARBO TALKS had and GARBO LAUGHS did. *Ninotchka* is a jewel of a comedy, and Garbo worked superbly with that master of subtle comedy, Ernst Lubitsch. *Ninotchka* brought her her last Academy Award nomination. She never won an Oscar, although she was first nominated in the 1929–30 season for both *Anna Christie* and *Romance*; in 1937, for *Camille*; and in 1939, for *Ninotchka*. In 1954, the Academy awarded her a special honorary Oscar for having brought magic to

266

the screen with her unforgettable performances. But these are, and will always be, the two flawless gems in her crown – the perfect romance, *Camille*; and the perfect comedy, *Ninotchka*.

I don't think she meant to withdraw permanently from the screen after the unfortunate *Two-Faced Woman*, which she liked as little as her director Cukor. They and the picture were victims of the new and fleeting morality code which ruined the lightweight comedy, making a heavy pudding out of what should have been a soufflé.

Eventually, MGM released her from any commitment owed them, because they could find no suitable vehicles for her. Actually, by the time World War Two was on, the international market, where she reigned as a top favourite, was lost to Hollywood. She might have made Daphne du Maurier's *My Cousin Rachel*, with Cukor directing, but she backed out, and so then did he. In the late forties she almost did another film with Cukor directing, playing Georges Sand, with Laurence Olivier as her leading man – but nothing came of that project. Selznick tried to interest her in starring as the lovely but deadly heroine of *The Paradine Case*, and at much the same time RKO commissioned Cukor to interest her in playing the Norwegian mother in *I Remember Mama*. She sent back the message: 'No murderesses; no mamas.'

The pictures she nearly did are almost legion. Zanuck did everything to interest her in *Anastasia*; she remained uninterested. Visconti wanted her recently for the film he has never made of Proust's 'Remembrance of Things Past'; some time ago, according to a Spanish magazine, Cukor found an original called *Sacrifice* which would have starred her with Alain Delon; but she turned it down, and it has never been made. Before that, Selznick had tried to interest her, and then Ingrid Bergman, in a picture about Sarah Bernhardt; she would not commit herself.

Only once did she actually sign to make a picture, which Walter Wanger was to produce abroad in Technicolor, an adaptation of Balzac's *La Duchesse de Langeais*, in which James Mason was to have been her leading man and Max Ophuls would have directed. She accepted a cheque and journeyed to Italy, where costume tests were shot of her in colour by William Daniels, James Wong Howe, and an unnamed Italian cinematographer, probably a Technicolor adviser. And then, suddenly, for reasons never satisfactorily explained Wanger's financial backing faded out, and he could not get new backers. James Mason has said that

Garbo herself was not co-operative about wooing the men with the money interests. Wanger disavowed that. I do know that Garbo was mortified when she learned that her name would no longer guarantee financial backing for a film starring her, for she told a close mutual friend, 'It's over. Never again.' It has come to the place where, when she agrees to read a screenplay, she has confessed that almost simultaneously she begins to think of good reasons why she should *not* do the script in question.*

Although she made frequent trips to Hollywood after her final picture, they were only business and social journeys. She once owned considerable real estate in Southern California, but has now reportedly sold most of it and invested the money in other securities in other parts of the world. She remains frugal, and is a rich woman in her own right. Once she had a coterie of friends in and around the film colony, but most of them have died or moved from the Pacific Coast. Only George Cukor, Rouben Mamoulian, and Gaylord Hauser are still on hand to receive her when she comes West.

Shortly after the debacle of *Two-Faced Woman*, she took up residence in New York City, and it was during the war years and subsequently right up to 1960, when I was frequently in Manhattan, that I would again catch glimpses of her around town.

I once went to an exclusive candy store, Altman & Kuhne, on Fifth Avenue, to buy a gift box. A woman wearing a fur coat and fur hat was ahead of me at the counter, her back thus to me. And then I heard her voice as she gave George Cukor's address as the place where the candy should be sent. It was the one and only voice. She turned, stared at me a brief second, the lids with those incredible lashes fluttering down over the high cheekbones, and then she went out alone into the brisk air.

In New York nobody bothers her; they respect her desire for privacy. As a matter of fact, only once in Southern California, when she was lunching at the Beverly Hills Hotel with a good friend, the late Virginia Burrowes, did I ever see somebody try to get her autograph. He was a

* The one big mystery remains: whatever happened to those colour tests she made in Italy? They would be the only colour film ever shot on Garbo. About twelve years ago in London, I asked Wanger about that film, and he merely shook his head sadly. 'I don't know what happened to it,' he said. 'Your guess is as good as mine.'

promising young actor, and should have known better. Garbo only ignored him, while Miss Burrowes coolly but firmly dealt with him. I've seen Garbo walk casually alone down Fifth Avenue or Madison, be recognised, and allowed to go her serene way. Admirers look, but don't speak – and, of course, never touch.

In Hollywood, as I say, she was not always so lucky. Quite by accident, I learned that her dentist, a big and very competent Swede, was also mine. I learned only because early one morning I left his office and went towards the elevator, just as the elevator doors opened and Garbo came out and went to his office. Sometime later on a subsequent visit, I said to the dentist. 'I didn't know Garbo was a patient of yours.' He looked at me over the tops of his glasses with big sad eyes. 'She used to be,' he said. 'It was that damned stupid girl who used to operate the elevator who ruined everything. She stopped the elevator between floors when Miss Garbo was her only passenger and told her how she idolised her and was crazy about her. Miss Garbo was terrified, persuaded her to bring the elevator down to street level, and then fled. She phoned me when she got home to say she was sorry but she could never come back to me. God damn that stupid elevator girl!'

On the other hand, a great-aunt of mine returning by ship to her native Sweden, used to pass Garbo, who was also a passenger, as they walked the promenade deck. To her pleasure and surprise, she was stopped one day by Garbo, who engaged her in conversation in Swedish. I've always thought that perhaps much of her withdrawal from strangers, especially in the beginning, stemmed not only from her natural distrust of them, but also a reluctance to speak in a language in which she did not spontaneously think; it's not easy to think in Swedish and simultaneously translate to speak in English, a difficult language at best for foreigners. She was, and still is, like many of her countrywomen, a very shy and extremely sensitive person, and few have ever got to know what a charming sense of humour and droll wit she often evinces when she's comfortable with those she knows.

She made a friend of Allen Porter, when he was in the Cinema Department of the Museum of Modern Art, and often sat alone or with him or some other close friend, viewing one of her films, especially run off for her. The Garbo up on the screen she never thought of in the first person; it was always 'she' or 'that girl'. Sometimes she even got her sexes confused, and the image became 'that fellow'. She would say, 'Watch that girl; she's about to do something rather interesting'; 'Oh, she wasn't very good in that scene, was she?' or 'That fellow sure does have a lot to learn.'

Once, walking down Madison Avenue, I saw her ahead of me, and I remained discreetly behind, stopping to look into store windows when she stopped, and moving on when she walked on, always lingering some yards behind whenever she paused at a street corner. Finally, the inevitable happened. She caught a green light, but by the time I got to the kerb, the light had changed to red and I had to wait. I saw her across the street as she paused. She half-turned with an amused little smile, lifted one gloved hand in farewell, as if to let me know that she had known all along that I was following her – and then went on her way, lost quickly in the milling crowd.

I made my first trip to Sweden early in 1959. Stockholm was redolent with its own dramatic history, but it became memorable to me because I found the places where Garbo had lived and worked when she was young before she became famous. Even when I left Stockholm, in the university town of Uppsala, there on a hill is the big castle where Queen Christina formally abdicated, renouncing the crown of Sweden as Garbo had so movingly done in her picture about Christina. But in old Stockholm, across the river, on the South Side (the Söder), now as it was then a tenement area with ancient cobblestoned streets, is Blekingegatan, 32. There on the third floor of this cold-water flat, in a four-room apartment, is the house where she was born on 18 September 1905, Greta Lovisa Gustafsson, the youngest daughter of an unskilled labourer, Karl Gustafsson, and his wife, *née* Anna Karlsson. She had an older sister, named Alva, with whom she was never as close as she was to the handsome brother, Sven, the middle child.

I don't know whether Blekingegatan, 32 still stands, as it did in 1959, nor do I know if there are still local barber-shops in the neighbourhood, as there still were then, very much like Arthur Ekengren's, where she went to work as a soap lather girl after her father died. I haunted the places where she once lived and worked, looking as one might look on Delos for some sign of Apollo or on the shores of the Cyprian Isle for some hint of Aphrodite rising from the sea foam.

At that time, in 1959, the department store known as

PUB offered for sale at a modest price a photocopy of her application for a job there. For years I had such a copy and noted on the form was that revealing statement: 'Reason for leaving: To enter the films' (naturally in Swedish). Thanks to PUB, she did some modelling of millinery there, and the door was opened to her for commercial films.

She was persuaded to try for acceptance as a student in the Royal Dramatic Academy of Sweden's own state theatre, the Royal Dramatic Theatre. She was accepted, and began her studies. More than anything else, she wanted to be a stage actress, and once anybody has seen a performance of a play at Sweden's Royal Dramatic Theatre, he can understand why: Sweden's national playhouse, like London's, is the home of some of the best acting in the world. Garbo, however, made only a few stage appearances in small supporting roles while she was learning her craft at the Academy: in a German comedy, *The Tortoise Shell*; as a lady's maid in J. M. Barrie's *The Admirable Crichton*; in a Russian drama, *Violins of Autumn*; as a prostitute in a Swedish drama, *The Invisible*; and in Jules Romain's French farce, *Knock*, or *The Triumph of Medicine*.

Outside of Stockholm in a suburb known as Rasunda are the offices of Svensk Filmindustri. From there, one day in the summer of 1923, a distinguished Russian-Jewish director, Mauritz Stiller, sent word to the Academy's director, Gustaf Molander, asking if two promising young female students could be sent over for a film he was going to make of Nobel Prize novelist Selma Lagerlöf's *Gösta Berling's Saga*. Molander sent a dark-haired girl, Mona Mårtensson, and the fair-haired Greta Gustafsson. Miss Mårtesson was signed almost at once for one of the principal roles. Stiller deliberated about the younger Greta Gustafsson, and when he sent for her to come to his home, he had already decided to use her and had almost decided to rename her 'Mona Gabór'. By the time Miss Gustafsson arrived, however, he had the name for her – Greta Garbo! She signed a contract to work for him as the Countess Elisabeth Dohna in *Gösta Berling's Saga* on 23 July, 1923. Stiller warned her. 'You'll have to reduce ten kilos.' She did. She did everything Stiller told her to do. Only once did she flare up in protest to cry with tears of rage, 'Damn you, Stiller, I hate you!' When Louis B. Mayer offered Stiller a director's contract at MGM, Stiller would sign only if the studio also signed his protégée, Greta Garbo, with whom he wanted to work. She was signed at a starting weekly salary of $350, and she arrived with Stiller in New York Harbour on board the 'Drottningholm' on 6 July, 1925, not quite two years after she had first signed a contract to work for him in films. Fate was not kind to Stiller at MGM; he was taken off every project he began there. Garbo, on the other hand, became the idol and the legend.

There is no doubt that Stiller taught her almost everything she knew about acting. He may have been Svengali to her Trilby, but when he could not adapt himself to the Hollywood ways of MGM, she, unlike Trilby, was able to go on alone, displaying for the camera all that he had taught her. Because of him, the camera became her friend and allowed her to be its most beloved mistress. From her first American film in 1926, she had of course a remarkable cinematographer, the late William Daniels, who photographed twenty of her MGM films. She was the perfect model for the instrument; he, its perfect master.

She has never forgotten Mauritz Stiller, however. How could she? Death has claimed others who were close to her, but death was especially quick to rob her of him who had made it all possible. In 1929, when she was making one of her silent films, *Wild Orchids*, she was in her dressing-room when the cablegram was delivered, bringing her word of Stiller's death in Sweden. For a moment, she nearly collapsed, but when concern was expressed, she quickly regained her composure and steeled herself to say, 'Tell them I'll be made up and ready to go on in twenty minutes.'

She is almost never lonely, although there are times when she prefers to be left alone, which is quite a different thing. There have been many friends and companions in her life, male and female. Even in the summer of 1972, aged sixty-seven, she was squired all over Italy by a handsome, well-to-do, thirty-two-year-old Neapolitan. She is not alone, unless she wants to be. But Mauritz Stiller was her great love and her first great loss. 'Damn you, Stiller, I hate you!' she may have said when he reduced her to tears while directing the only picture they ever made together, but she always openly worshipped him.

Earlier this spring, the front page of *The Daily Telegraph* in London headlined a story that Greta Garbo was a patient in a Barcelona hospital, where she had undergone a successful operation twelve days previously for cataracts in both eyes, which had threatened her with blindness.

I like best to think of her as she was on one of the last days I caught a glimpse of her. It was in New York, on a

Garbo in repose – a delightful study from As You Desire Me *(1932)*

spring day with showers. I was waiting, as before, for a signal light to change on Fifth Avenue at 57th Street, and suddenly I saw her on the other side of the street. She was with another woman. She was wearing a shiny blue belted raincoat, and her companion, a green one. The signal changed, and I stepped aside to wait, as the two women crossed the street, laughing and talking gaily like very young schoolgirls. I watched them go west on 57th towards a favourite ice cream parlour – and then I realised that beside me was a middle-aged woman, from the Bronx or perhaps Brooklyn, who was also looking at them. She turned to inquire of me, 'That was Greta Garbo, wasn't it?'

I nodded. 'Yes, it was.'

She looked down at the solemn-faced young boy she held by the hand. 'You see now,' she said, 'I been telling you not to stay indoors all the time. You go out, and who knows? You might see Greta Garbo!'

APPENDIX

Ever since 1941 when Garbo completed work on *Two-Faced Woman*, scarcely a year has passed without rumours of her return to the screen. Although it now seems evident that she did not initially intend that picture to be her finale, fate conspired to prevent her ever appearing before the cameras again. Certainly, over the years which followed there were scripts, stories and ideas aplenty offered to her: some she took seriously, others she rejected out of hand. But clearly there remained a desire in her to film again *if* the right picture and the right working conditions ever materialised.

Anyone who has ever doubted Garbo's right to be called a legend has only to consider the excitement that has been generated whenever the chance that she might come out of retirement has made headlines, to see just how wrong such misgivings are. What other star could claim not to have entered a film studio for over forty years and yet can still set the world's pulse tingling at the mere thought that she just *might* act again?

The projects which have been linked with Garbo's name have varied from the intriguing to the quite obviously ridiculous, but I have felt it was worthwhile in a book such as this to list the 'comebacks that never came'. Aside from these specific proposals, there were a number of other ideas apparently put to her, but as the details are so sparse or contradictory I have decided to leave them out. For the record, though, we do know that Garbo herself expressed a desire at various times to play Salome, Madame Bovary and even Hamlet. She was very taken with Daryl Zanuck's plan to have her star in *Anastasia*, and discussed at length with Aldous Huxley the idea of playing St Francis of Assisi. She also gave a lot of thought to a Spanish story, *Sacrifice*, brought to her by George Cukor. (It was Cukor who said that after withdrawing from *My Cousin Rachel* – listed hereunder – Garbo explained her reluctance to return to the screen at that time with the words, 'I can't go through with it. I have not the courage to make another picture.')

It is interesting, too, to note how many *male* roles Garbo contemplated playing, and several critics have remarked on her androgynous quality. Cecil Beaton was particularly struck by this quality and wrote in his *Self-Portrait With Friends* (1973): 'I could see Greta wearing velvet trousers and smoking a cigar. From Joan of Arc to Christina of Sweden, the idea of women in cavalier clothes had a visual aspect that was appealing to her; she would have liked to play St Francis of Assisi, also Lorenzaccio and Dorian Gray. "*Travesti*" has obviously titillated her, and, since early days,

The Single Standard *(1929)*

she has enjoyed wearing the more romantic of men's apparel in her films. Ventriloquists' dolls and pierrots possess an ambiguity that delights her sense of the perverse. This is, no doubt, the reason why stories have been circulated about her having odd tendencies.'

Here, then, are the films that Garbo never made: some of them replete with the kind of possibilities that would surely have drawn great performances from her. Sadly, we can now only relish them in the cinema of the imagination.

1942

The Girl From Leningrad
Garbo was to play a Russian Resistance Fighter in Nazi-occupied territory. MGM signed a contract with her in December 1942 for $70,000 – but she found the script 'depressing' and the film was cancelled.

1943

The Violent Seas
Garbo was to be featured as the woman skipper of a Norwegian merchant navy ship. She liked the script, but negotiations never got beyond the preliminary stage.

1944

Madame Curie
MGM had bought the rights to the life story of the Nobel Prize winning scientist in 1939 and again tried unavailingly to interest Garbo in the role.

1945

The Picture of Dorian Gray
Producer Albert Lewin offered Garbo the lead role in a film of Oscar Wilde's classic story. She turned it down, and young actor Hurd Hatfield found fame as the aristocrat whose beauty is unmarked by depravity while his portrait progressively decays.

1945

Flesh and the Devil
MGM propose a remake of Garbo's 1926 hit – but she vetoes the idea. She was said to be more interested in playing Anna Lucasta and had tried without success to buy the film rights.

1946

Sarah Bernhardt
David Selznick announces that Garbo is to replace Ingrid Bergman in life story of the famous French actress: but the project founders.

1946

Saint Joan
Garbo invited to play title role in British film of George Bernard Shaw's play. But producer Gabriel Pascal failed to raise necessary finance.

1947

The Paradine Case
David Selznick again tries to coax Garbo back onto the screen to play a woman poisoner.

1947

I Remember Mama
George Cukor and RKO try to interest Garbo in playing this story of a stouthearted Norwegian mother. She sends the same cable to Cukor and David Selznick: 'No murderesses; no mamas.'

1947

A Streetcar Named Desire
Garbo offered the role of Blanche in Tennessee Williams' play now to be filmed. She turns it down. 'I'm too direct and too masculine,' she says. 'I couldn't bear to tell lies and see things round corners like that girl.'

1948

The Eagle With Two Heads
Alexander Korda makes plans to film this Jean Cocteau play after Garbo declares, 'It is the only thing I would like to do. It has an atmosphere that appeals to me, and I've always wanted to play Elizabeth of Austria.' Again the idea comes to nothing.

1948

Inconnue de la Seine
Billy Wilder tries to interest Garbo in the story of a drowned girl reconstructing her life, inspired by the famous death mask in the Louvre. She declines, and when asked if there is any part she *would* play in a comeback, replies, 'A clown. A male clown.'

1949

Garbo as the 'star' of a comic strip from the Italian publication Bombolo, 28 February 1935

La Duchesse de Langeais
(a.k.a. *Lover and Friend*)
Garbo actually signs a contract to make an Italian/US version of this Balzac story in Rome for producer Walter Wan-

ger, with Max Ophuls as director and James Mason as co-star. Costume tests were actually shot by William Daniels (the only colour film ever taken of her), but the loss of financial backing caused Wanger to cancel the film. Returning to America, Garbo said, 'It's over. Never again.'

1949

The Lady in the Iron Mask
Producer Dore Schary proposes this costume drama variation on the famous French legend of a man in an iron mask, but fails to raise any enthusiasm from Garbo.

1949

Georges Sand
Garbo reportedly interested by George Cukor in playing in life story of the remarkable French authoress. Laurence Olivier, who lost out to John Gilbert in *Queen Christina*, would be co-star. But she declines gracefully: 'Georges Sand could make a wonderful story, but it's eight years since my last film; the war came in the meantime and there are such difficulties in the world today.'

1950

Inspiration
MGM again suggest Garbo remake one of her earlier hits, with Montgomery Clift taking the role played by Robert Montgomery. She is not interested.

1951

Strictly Dishonourable
Garbo returns to the screen! Or to be more precise several sequences from *A Woman of Affairs* featuring her and John Gilbert are shown as part of Ezio Pinza's new film. Her voice is also heard during a two-minute trailer for a film called *The River*.

1951

St Teresa
Salvador Dali announces that Garbo will star in a film he is preparing of the life of the Spanish mystic St Teresa of Avila who claimed to see visions and founded a new order of nuns. Nothing further is heard.

1952

My Cousin Rachel
George Cukor tried to get her to star opposite Richard Burton in the film of Daphne du Maurier's book. She declined

278

saying 'I could never be Cornish' and the part went to Olivia de Havilland. Richard Burton later met Garbo and asked permission to kiss her knee – which she granted. 'It was an experience I'll never forget,' he said afterwards.

1956

Modjeska: Her Life and Loves
Garbo agrees to make a comeback – but on the stage in a play by Antoni Gronowicz about the Polish actress, Helena Modjeska, whose career and introspective personality closely resembled that of Garbo. Sadly, she never made her Broadway debut.

1957

Phedra
Press stories that Garbo is to mime the role of Phedra in a new ballet to be staged in Paris. Music by Georges Auric, words by Jean Cocteau, and choreography by Serge Lifar. When the excitement dies down, the part goes to Tamara Toumanova.

1958

The Miracle
Director Irving Rapper says that Garbo wishes to play the role of a Mother Superior in a remake of this picture first made just after World War I. He tells pressmen, 'Miss Garbo made the initial approach. I was very excited when I learned of her interest. I believe she would like the part, and she would be perfect for it.' But once again nothing materialised.

1959

Le Testament d'Orphée
Jean Cocteau invites Garbo to appear in a short scene with Picasso in his surrealist film. She declines, telling him: 'Film producers want me to do today what I did before in order that people will say I can no longer do it.'

1960

The Deep Blue Sea
Another combined effort by MGM and George Cukor to get Garbo to return in a film based on Terrence Rattigan's play. She shows no interest, nor in the life story of the actress Eleanora Duse.

A Swedish newspaper cartoon from Svenska Dagbladet, *where Garbo remained a favourite daughter*

1963

Death Be Not Proud

Italian actor Rossano Brazzi tells the press he is to appear with Garbo in a film of John Gunther's novel, written in 1949, which David Lean will direct. It will be shot in London and Italy. 'Miss Garbo's role,' he says, 'is very romantic and suits her well. It is not a role for a young woman.' But the fifty-eight-year-old Garbo never confirms or denies the story.

1963

The Silence

Ingmar Bergman asks Garbo to appear in this picture which would have been her first Swedish-speaking role. Although they discuss the part at length, nothing materialises.

1969

The Phynx

Garbo is offered a cameo role in this comedy about four youngsters to be produced by Warner Bros. Although three other veteran actors from Hollywood's past, Xavier Cugat, Ruby Keeler and Leo Gorcey, do appear, Garbo wisely declined her specially written part.

1971

A la Recherche du Temps Perdu
(Remembrance of Things Past)

Luchino Visconti announces that Garbo has approached him to play the small part of Queen Sophia of Naples. Also said to be in the cast are Sir Laurence Olivier (fated never to act with her), Marlon Brando, Alain Delon and Madelina Renaud. Again, though, there is no return in this Marcel Proust classic.

1980

Mother Theresa

Rumours reach the press that Garbo, now seventy-four, is at last prepared to film again and make the life-story of the great humanitarian Mother Theresa. She is said to be prepared to donate any money she makes from the film to help her subject's work in India. As with every other 'comeback', further details have never been forthcoming . . .

FILMOGRAPHY

1920

The Gay Cavalier (a.k.a. *En Lyckoriddare*)
Skandia Films. Produced and directed by John Brunius.
Starring: Eugene Nifford.
(Greta and her sister, Alva, played uncredited extras in a
dance sequence.)

1921

How Not to Dress
PUB Department Store. Produced by Harse W. Tullborgs.
Directed by Captain Ragnar Ring.
Starring: Olga Anderson. With Greta Gustafsson.
Our Daily Bread
Stockholm Consumers' Co-operative Association. Pro-
duced by Fribergs Filmbyre.
Directed by Captain Ragnar Ring.
Starring: Lars Hanson. With Greta Gustafsson.

1922

Peter the Tramp (a.k.a. *Luffar-Petter*)
Erik A. Petschler Production. Directed and written by Erik
A. Petschler.
Starring: Erik A. Petschler, Helmer Larsson, Frederik
Olsson, Tyra Ryman, Gucken Cederborg, Greta Gus-
tafsson.

1924

The Story of Gösta Berling (a.k.a. *Gösta Berling's Saga*)
Svensk Filmindustri. Directed by Mauritz Stiller. Written
by Mauritz Stiller and Ragnar Hylten-Cavallius from the
novel *Gostä Berling's Saga* by Selma Lagerlof.
Starring: Lars Hanson, Greta Garbo, Ellen Cederstrom,

Mona Martenson, Gerda Lundequist, Torsten Kammeren.
The Odalisque from Smolny
Svensk Filmindustri-Trianon Films joint production. Written and directed by Mauritz Stiller.
Starring: Greta Garbo, Einar Hanson.
(Only some location shots in Constantinople were made for this projected film, abandoned because of lack of finance.)

1925

The Street of Sorrow (a.k.a. *The Joyless Street*)
A Sofar-Film. Directed by G. W. Pabst. Written by Willy Haas from the novel, *Die Freudlose Gasse* by Hugo Bettauer.
Starring: Werner Krauss, Asta Nielson, Jaro Furth, Greta Garbo, Agnes Esterhazy, Einar Hanson, Loni Nest, Marlene Dietrich.

1926

The Torrent
MGM. Directed by Monta Bell. Written by Dorothy Farnum from the novel, *Entre Naranjos* by Vicente Blasco-Ibanez.
Starring: Ricardo Cortez, Greta Garbo, Gertrude Olmstead, Edward Connelly, Tully Marshall, Mack Swain, Mario Carillo.
The Temptress
MGM. Directed by Fred Niblo. (Also Mauritz Stiller, uncredited.) Written by Dorothy Farnum from the novel, *La Tierra de Todos* by Vicente Blasco-Ibanez.
Starring: Antonio Moreno, Greta Garbo, Marc MacDermott, Lionel Barrymore, Armand Kaliz, Robert Anderson, Virginia Brown Faire, Inez Gomez.

1927

Flesh and the Devil
MGM. Directed by Clarence Brown. Written by Benjamin F. Glazer from the novel *The Undying Past* by Hermann Sudermann.
Starring: John Gilbert, Greta Garbo, Lars Hanson, Barbara Kent, William Orlamund, George Fawcett, Marc MacDermott, Marcelle Corday.
Love
MGM. Directed by Edmund Goulding. Written by Frances Marion from the novel, *Anna Karenina* by Leo Tolstoy.
Starring: John Gilbert, Greta Garbo, George Fawcett, Emily Fitzroy, Brandon Hurst, Philippe de Lacy.

1928

The Divine Woman
MGM. Directed by Victor Seastrom. Written by Dorothy Farnum from the play *Starlight* by Gladys Unger with additional work by Victor Seastrom and Frances Marion.
Starring: Greta Garbo, Lars Hanson, Lowell Sherman, Polly Moran, Dorothy Cumming, John Mack Brown, Paulette Duval.

The Mysterious Lady
MGM. Directed by Fred Niblo. Written by Bess Meredyth from the novel, *War in the Dark* by Ludwig Wolff.
Starring: Greta Garbo, Conrad Nagel, Gustav von Seyffertitz, Edward Connelly, Albert Pollet, Richard Alexander.

1929

A Woman of Affairs
MGM. Directed by Clarence Brown. Written by Bess Meredyth from the novel, *The Green Hat* by Michael Arlen.
Starring: Greta Garbo, John Gilbert, Lewis Stone, John Mack Brown, Douglas Fairbanks Jr, Hobart Bosworth, Dorothy Sebastian.

Wild Orchids
MGM. Directed by Sidney Franklin. Written by Willis Goldbeck from an original screen story, *Heat* by John Colton.
Starring: Greta Garbo, Lewis Stone, Nils Asther.

The Single Standard
MGM. Directed by John S. Robertson. Written by Josephine Lovett from the novel, *The Single Standard* by Adela Rogers St John.
Starring: Greta Garbo, Nils Asther, John Mack Brown, Dorothy Sebastian, Lane Chandler, Robert Castle, Kathlyn Williams.

The Kiss
MGM. Directed by Jacques Feyder. Written by Hans Kraly from an original screen story, *The Kiss* by George M. Saville.
Starring: Greta Garbo, Conrad Nagel, Anders Randolf, Holmes Herbert, Lew Ayres, George Davis.

1930

Anna Christie
MGM. Directed by Clarence Brown. Written by Frances Marion from the play, *Anna Christie* by Eugene O'Neill.
Starring: Greta Garbo, Charles Bickford, George F. Marion, Marie Dressler, James T. Mack, Lee Phelps.

Romance
MGM. Directed by Clarence Brown. Written by Bess Meredyth and Edwin Justus Mayer from the play, *Romance* by Edward Sheldon.
Starring: Greta Garbo, Lewis Stone, Gavin Gordon, Elliott Nugent, Florence Lake, Clare Blandick, Countess de Liguoro.

1931

Inspiration
MGM. Directed by Clarence Brown. Written by Gene Markey based on his own original screen story.
Starring: Greta Garbo, Robert Montgomery, Lewis Stone, Marjorie Rambeau, Edwin Maxwell, Oscar Apfel, Joan Marsh, Karen Morley, Richard Tucker.

Susan Lennox: Her Fall and Rise (a.k.a. *The Rise of Helga*)
MGM. Directed by Robert Z. Leonard. Written by Wanda Tuchock from the novel, *Susan Lennox* by David Graham Phillips.
Starring: Greta Garbo, Clark Gable, Jean Hersholt, John Miljan, Alan Hale, Hale Hamilton, Cecil Cunningham, Marjorie King, Ian Keith.

1932

Mata Hari
MGM. Directed by George Fitzmaurice. Written by Benjamin Glazer and Leo Birinski based on their original story.
Starring: Greta Garbo, Ramon Novarro, Lional Barrymore, Lewis Stone, C. Henry Gordon, Karen Morley, Edmund Breese, Frank Reicher.

Grand Hotel
MGM. Directed by Edmund Goulding. Written by William A. Drake from the play *Grand Hotel* by Vicki Baum.
Starring: Greta Garbo, John Barrymore, Joan Crawford, Wallace Beery, Lionel Barrymore, Lewis Stone, Jean Hersholt, Tully Marshall, Frank Conroy, Edwin Maxwell.

As You Desire Me
MGM. Directed by George Fitzmaurice. Written by Gene Markey from the play, *As You Desire Me* by Luigi Pirandello.
Starring: Greta Garbo, Melvyn Douglas, Erich von Stroheim, Owen Moore, Hedda Hopper, Rafaela Ottiano, Roland Varno.

1933

Queen Christina
MGM. Directed by Rouben Mamoulian. Written by Salka Viertel based on her original screen story with additional work by Margaret F. Levin, H. M. Harwood and S. N. Behrman.
Starring: Greta Garbo, John Gilbert, Ian Keith, Lewis Stone, Elizabeth Young, C. Aubrey Smith, Reginald Owen, Gustav von Seyffertitz, George Renevent.

1934

The Painted Veil
MGM. Directed by Richard Boleslawski. Written by Salka Viertel, John Meehan and Edith Fitzgerald from the novel, *The Painted Veil* by W. Somerset Maugham.
Starring: Greta Garbo, Herbert Marshall, George Brent, Warner Oland, Jean Hersholt, Beulah Bondi, Katherine Alexander, Cecilia Parker, Forrester Harvey, Soo Yong.

1935

Anna Karenina
MGM. Directed by Clarence Brown. Written by Salka Viertel, Clemence Dane and S. N. Behrman from the novel, *Anna Karenina* by Leo Tolstoy.
Starring: Greta Garbo, Fredric March, Basil Rathbone, Freddie Bartholomew, Maureen O'Sullivan, May Robson, Reginald Owen, Joan Marsh, Harry Allen, Mary Forbes.

1937

Camille
MGM. Directed by George Cukor. Written by Zoe Akins, Frances Marion and James Hilton from the play and novel, *La Dame aux Camellias* by Alexandre Dumas.
Starring: Greta Garbo, Robert Taylor, Lionel Barrymore, Elizabeth Allen, Henry Daniell, Rex O'Malley, E. E. Clive, Marion Ballou, Joan Brodel, Fritz Leiber Jr.
Conquest (a.k.a. *Marie Walewska*)
MGM. Directed by Clarence Brown. Written by Salka Viertel, Samuel Hoffenstein and S. N. Behrman from the novel, *Pani Walewska* by Waclaw Gasiorowski and a dramatisation by Helen Jerome.
Starring: Greta Garbo, Charles Boyer, Reginald Owen, Alan Marshall, Henry Stephenson, Leif Erickson, Dame May Whitty, C. Henry Gordon, Maria Ouspenskaya.

1939

Ninotchka
MGM. Directed by Ernst Lubitsch. Written by Charles Brackett, Billy Wilder and Walter Reisch from an original story by Melchior Lengyel.
Starring: Greta Garbo, Melvyn Douglas, Ina Claire, Bela Lugosi, Sig Ruman, Felix Bressart, Alexander Granach, Edwin Maxwell, Richard Carle.

1941

Two-Faced Woman
MGM. Directed by George Cukor. Written by Salka Viertel, S. N. Behrman and George Oppenheimer from the play, *Two-Faced Woman* by Ludwig Fulda.
Starring: Greta Garbo, Melvyn Douglas, Constance Bennett, Roland Young, Robert Sterling, Ruth Gordon, Francis Carson.

ACKNOWLEDGMENTS

This book has been made possible by the special access which I was granted to the huge files of material on Garbo held by the Swedish Film Institute in Stockholm, the American Film Institute in New York, and the British Film Institute in London. In particular, I found the series of scrapbooks donated to the BFI by an anonymous Garbo fan and collected during her actual working period, of enormous value: several of the articles in this book are in fact taken from their pages.

I should also like to acknowledge the contributions of the following: Lars Hanson, John Gilbert, Nils Asther, Clark Gable, Ramon Navarro, Lionel Barrymore, John Barrymore, Fredric March, Charles Boyer, Melvyn Douglas, Sally Ekengren, Carl Brisson, Eugene Nifford, Victor Seastrom, Val Lewton, Sven-Hugo Borg, Pola Negri, Wilhelm Sörensen, John Loder, Cecil Beaton, Clarence Brown, William Daniels, Lord Olivier, Rouben Mamoulian, Cecilia Parker, Tallulah Bankhead, Basil Rathbone, Robert Taylor, George Cukor and DeWitt Bodeen. I am also grateful to the following newspapers and magazines for their permission to quote material from their pages: *Film Monthly*, *Film Weekly*, *Motion Picture Magazine*, *Sunday Express*, *Biografbladlet*, *A/B Svensk Filmindustri*, *New York Herald*, Associated Newspapers, *Photoplay Magazine*, *American Film*, *Film Pictorial*, *Picturegoer*, *Film World*, *Los Angeles Times-Mirror* and *Focus on Film*. Film stills have also been generously provided by the British Film Institute, MGM Pictures, Svensk Filmindustri and Sofar Films.